HSC

ALLEN COUNTY PUBLIC LIBRARY

P9-BIL-482

381.1 B72I
Brady, Marni Ayers.
Internet in an hour for
  shoppers & bargain hunters

Internet in an Hour for Shoppers & Bargain Hunters

Marni Ayers Brady

Monique Peterson

Don Mayo

Kathy Berkemeyer

Acknowledgements

Allen County Public Library
900 Webster Street
PO Box 2270
Fort Wayne, IN 46801-2270

To my brother, JR, whose laughter has always brightened my path.

Marni Ayers Brady

Thanks Imelda, you've been an inspiration to us all.

Monique Peterson

To my family of friends—thanks for everything.

Don Mayo

Dedicated to the memory of my parents, John and Gert Madden.

Kathy Berkemeyer

Managing Editor	Technical and English Editors	Design and Layout	Cover Design and Layout
Jennifer Frew	Jennifer Frew	Midori Nakamura	Amy Capuano
	Monique Peterson	Shu Chen	
	Marni Ayers Brady	Maria Kardasheva	**Illustrations**
	Cathy Vesecky	Paul Wray	Ryan Sather

Copyright© 1999 by DDC Publishing, Inc.
Published by DDC Publishing, Inc.
The information contained herein is copyrighted by DDC Publishing, Inc.
All right reserved, including the right to reproduce this book or portions thereof in any form whatsoever. For information, address DDC Publishing, Inc., 275 Madison Avenue, 12ᵗʰ Floor, New York, New York 10016
Internet address: *http://www.ddcpub.com*

ISBN: 1-56243-697-X
Cat. No. HR9
DDC Publishing, Inc. Printing:
10 9   8   7   6   5   4   3   2   1
Printed in the United States of America.

Internet in an Hour is a trademark of DDC Publishing, Inc.
The DDC banner design is a registered trademark of DDC Publishing, Inc.

Netscape™, Netscape™ Communications logo, Netscape™ Communications Corporation, Netscape™ Communications, and Netscape™ Navigator are all trademarks of Netscape™ Communications Corporation.
Microsoft® and Windows® are registered trademarks of the Microsoft Corporation.
Yahoo!™ and Yahoo™ logo are trademarks of Yahoo!™
LYCOS™, LYCOS™ logo are trademarks of LYCOS™.
AltaVista™ and the AltaVista™ logo are trademarks of AltaVista Technology, Inc.
Digital™ and the Digital™ logo are trademarks of Digital Equipment Corporation.
Excite is a service mark of Excite Inc.
Some illustrations in this book and on the DDC Web site have been acquired from Web sites and are used for demonstration and educational purposes only. Online availability of text and images does not imply that they may be reused without the permission of the copyright holder, although the Copyright Act does permit certain unauthorized reuse as fair use under 17 U.S.C. Section 107

All registered trademarks, trademarks, and service marks are the property of their respective companies.

Contents

Introduction

This Book is Designed for You . . .

if you are ready to explore the World Wide Web of shopping! You'll learn how to get online and get the search results you want quickly. Find answers to all your questions about how you can shop safely and securely online and still find all the best bargains.

Internet in an Hour for Shoppers and Bargain Hunters is divided into three main sections: Basics, Shop the Web, and 101 Shopping Sites.

Basics

In Internet Basics, you can learn how to:

- Use Netscape Navigator to browse the World Wide Web.
- Use Internet Explorer to browse the World Wide Web.
- Access the Internet using America Online.
- Find information on the Web with search engines.

Shop the Web

In Shop the Web, you'll learn where to "window shop" first to find out what's for sale online. Learn how to browse for goods and comparison shop for the best prices before you spend money. Visit specialty shops and discover alternative ways to find great deals. Finally, know your options about how to spend money online safely and securely.

101 Shopping Sites

Each 101 Shopping Sites topic showcases Web sites where you're sure to get bottom-dollar deals. Learn where to go to save anywhere from 10–90% off retail prices and even get things for free.

What Do I Need to Use This Book?

This book assumes that you have some general knowledge and experience with computers and that you already know how to perform the following tasks:

- Use a mouse (double-click, etc.).
- Make your way around Microsoft Windows 95.
- Install and run programs.

If you are completely new to computers as well as the World Wide Web, you may want to refer to DDC's **Learning Microsoft Windows 95** or **Learning the Internet**.

This book also assumes that you have an Internet connection and access to browser applications such as Microsoft Internet Explorer 4.0, Netscape Navigator 4.0, or America Online.

✔ *If you do not currently have these applications, contact your Internet Service Provider for instructions on how to download them. You can also use other browsers or previous versions such as Explorer 3.0 and Navigator 3.0 to browse the Web.*

✔ *This book does not cover how to get connected to the Internet.*

Please read over the following list of "must haves" to ensure that you are ready to be connected to the Internet.

- A computer (with a recommended minimum of 16 MB of RAM) and a modem port.
- A modem (with a recommended minimum speed of 14.4kbps, and suggested speed of 28.8kbps) that is connected to an analog phone line (assuming you are not using a direct Internet connection through a school, corporation, etc.).
- Established access to the Internet through an online service, independent Internet Service Provider, etc.
- A great deal of patience. The Internet is a fun and exciting place, but getting connected can be frustrating at times. Expect to run into occasional glitches, get disconnected from time to time, or experience occasional difficulty in viewing certain Web pages and features. The more up-to-date your equipment and software are, however, the less difficulty you will probably experience.

Internet Cautions

ACCURACY:

- Be cautious not to believe everything on the Internet. Almost anyone can publish information on the Internet, and since there is no Internet editor or monitor, some information may be false. All information found on the World Wide Web should be checked for accuracy through additional reputable sources.

SECURITY:

- When sending information over the Internet, be prepared to let the world have access to it. Computer hackers can find ways to access anything that you send to anyone over the Internet, including e-mail. Be cautious when sending confidential information to anyone.

VIRUSES:

- These small, usually destructive computer programs hide inside of innocent-looking programs. Once a virus is executed, it attaches itself to other programs. When triggered, often by the occurrence of a date or time on the computer's internal clock/calendar, it executes a nuisance or damaging function, such as displaying a message on your screen, corrupting your files, or reformatting your hard disk.

B A S I C S

Netscape Navigator: 1

◆ About Netscape Navigator
◆ Start Netscape Navigator ◆ The Netscape Screen
◆ Exit Netscape Navigator

About Netscape Navigator

- This chapter focuses on Netscape Navigator 4.0, the Internet browser component of Netscape Communicator.

Start Netscape Navigator

1. Click the Start button ![Start].
2. Click Programs, Netscape Communicator, Netscape Navigator.
   OR

   If you have a shortcut to Netscape Communicator ![Netscape Communicator] on your desktop, double-click it to start Netscape Navigator.

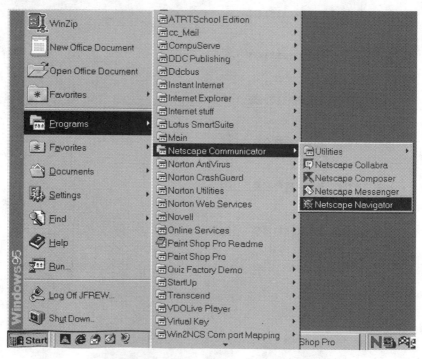

✔ *The first time you start Netscape Communicator, the New Profile Setup dialog box appears. Enter e-mail and service provider information in the dialog boxes that appear. If you don't know the information, you can leave it blank until you are ready to fill it in.*

The Netscape Screen

■ The Netscape Navigator screen contains features that help you explore the Internet. Some of these features are constant and some change depending on the task attempted or completed.

Title bar

Displays the name of the program (Netscape) and the current Web page (Welcome to Netscape).

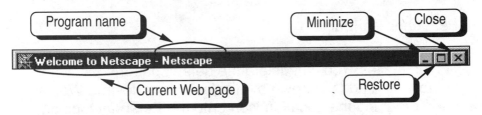

Menu bar

Displays drop-down lists of Netscape commands.

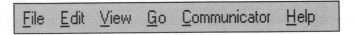

Navigation toolbar

Contains buttons for online activity. The name and icon on each button identify the command.

✔ *If the toolbar buttons are not visible, open the View menu and click Show Navigation Toolbar.*

Location toolbar

The electronic address of the current Web page displays in the Location field. You can also type the Web page address, called a Uniform Resource Locator (URL), in the Location field and press Enter to access it.

✔ *If the Location toolbar is not visible, open the View menu and click Show Location Toolbar.*

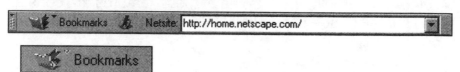

The Bookmarks QuickFile button is also on the Location toolbar. Click to view a list of sites that you have bookmarked for quick access. (For more on Bookmarks, see page 12.)

Personal toolbar

Contains buttons or links that you add to connect to your favorite sites. You can delete the default buttons (shown below) and add your own by displaying the desired Web site and dragging the Location icon onto the Personal toolbar.

Netscape's status indicator

Netscape's icon pulses when Netscape is processing a command. Click to return to Netscape's home page.

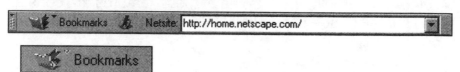

Status bar

When a Web page is opening, the Status bar indicates the downloading progress and the security level of the page being loaded. When you place the cursor over a hyperlink, the Status bar displays the URL of the link.

Component toolbar

The buttons on this toolbar link to other Netscape components: Navigator, Messenger Mailbox, Collabra Discussions, and Page Composer.

Exit Netscape Navigator

- Exiting Netscape Navigator and disconnecting from your Internet Service Provider (ISP) are two separate steps. You can disconnect from your service provider and still have Netscape Navigator open. You can also disconnect from Navigator and still have your ISP open.

- You may want to disconnect from your ISP and keep Netscape open to:

  - Read information obtained from the Web

  - Access information stored on your hard disk using Netscape

  - Compose e-mail to send later

- If you don't disconnect from your ISP and you pay an hourly rate, you will continue incurring charges.

  ✔ *You can disconnect from your ISP and still view Web information accessed during the current session by using the Back and Forward toolbar buttons. Your computer stores the visited sites in its memory.*

Netscape Navigator: 2

◆ The Navigation Toolbar
◆ Open World Wide Web Sites

The Navigation Toolbar

- The Netscape Navigation toolbar displays buttons for Netscape's most commonly used commands. Note that each button contains an icon and a word describing the button's function. Choosing any of these buttons activates the indicated task immediately.

- If the Navigation toolbar is not visible, select Show Navigation Toolbar from the View menu.

 Moves back through pages previously displayed. Back is available only if you have moved around among Web pages in the current Navigator session; otherwise, it is dimmed.

 Moves forward through pages previously displayed. Forward is available only if you have used the Back button; otherwise, it is dimmed.

 Reloads the currently displayed Web page. Use this button if the current page is taking too long to display or to update the current page with any changes that may have occurred since the page was downloaded.

 Displays the home page.

 Displays Netscape's Net Search Page. You can select one of several search tools from this page.

 Displays a menu with helpful links to Internet sites that contain search tools and services.

Prints the displayed page, topic, or article.

 Displays security information for the displayed Web page as well as information on Netscape security features.

 Stops the loading of a Web page.

Open World Wide Web Sites

- There are several ways to access a Web site. If you know the site's address, you can enter the correct Web address (URL) on the Location field on the Location toolbar.

- If the address you are entering is the address of a site you have visited recently or that you have bookmarked (see page 12 for more information on Bookmarks), you will notice as you begin to type the address that Netscape attempts to complete it for you. If the address that Netscape suggests is the one you want, press Enter.

- If the address that Netscape suggests is not correct, keep typing to complete the desired address and then press Enter. Or, you can click the down arrow next to the Location field to view a list of other possible matches, select an address, and press Enter.

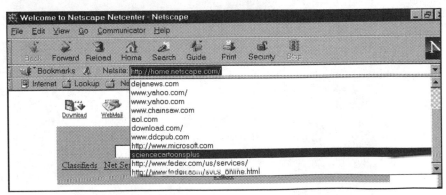

- There are a couple of shortcuts for entering URL addresses. One shortcut involves omitting the **http://www**. prefix from the Web address. Netscape assumes the **http://** protocol and the **www** that indicates that the site is located on the Web.

- If you are trying to connect to a company Web site, entering the company name is generally sufficient. Netscape assumes the **.com** suffix. For example, entering **ddcpublishing** on the location line and pressing Enter would reach the **http://www.ddcpub.com** address.

  ✔ *Don't be discouraged if you can't connect to the World Wide Web site immediately. The site may be offline temporarily. The site may also be very busy with other users trying to access it. Be sure the URL is typed accurately. Occasionally, it takes several tries to connect to a site.*

Netscape Navigator: 3

◆ History List ◆ Bookmarks ◆ Add Bookmarks
◆ Delete Bookmarks ◆ Print Web Pages

History List

- While you move back and forth among Web sites, Netscape automatically records each of these site locations in a History list, which is temporarily stored on your computer.

- You can use the History list to track or view sites that you have recently visited. The History list is an easy way to see the path you followed to get to a particular Web page.

- To view the History list, click History on the Communicator menu, or press Ctrl+H. To link to a site shown in the History list, double-click on it.

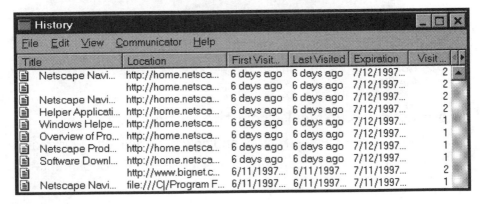

Bookmarks

- A Bookmark is a placeholder containing the title and URL of a Web page that, when selected, links directly to that page. If you find a Web site that you like and want to revisit, you can create a Bookmark to record its location. (See **Add Bookmarks** on the following page.)

- The Netscape Bookmark feature maintains permanent records of the Web sites in your Bookmark files so that you can return to them easily.

- You can view the Bookmarks menu by selecting Bookmarks from the Communicator menu or by clicking on the Bookmarks QuickFile button 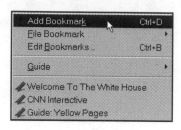 on the Location toolbar. The drop-down menu shown below appears.

Add Bookmark	Ctrl+D
File Bookmark	▶
Edit Bookmarks ..	Ctrl+B
Guide	▶
Welcome To The White House	
CNN Interactive	
Guide: Yellow Pages	

Add Bookmarks

To add a Bookmark from an open Web page:

- Display the Web page to add, go to Bookmarks on the Communicator menu and click Add Bookmark.

Add Bookmark	Ctrl+D
File Bookmark	▶
Edit Bookmarks...	Ctrl+B

✔ *Netscape does not confirm that a bookmark has been added to the file.*

To create a Bookmark from the History list:

1. Click Communicator, History and select the listing to bookmark.
2. Right-click on your selection and choose Add To Bookmarks from the pop-up menu.

Delete Bookmarks

- Bookmarks may be deleted at anytime. For example, you may wish to delete a Bookmark if a Web site no longer exists or is no longer of interest to you.

To delete a Bookmark:

1. Click Communicator.
2. Click Bookmarks.
3. Click Edit Bookmarks.

3 1822 03566 0627

4. In the Bookmarks window, select the Bookmark you want to delete by clicking on it from the Bookmark list.

5. Press the Delete key.

OR

Right-click on the Bookmark and select <u>D</u>elete Bookmark from the pop-up menu as shown in the following illustration.

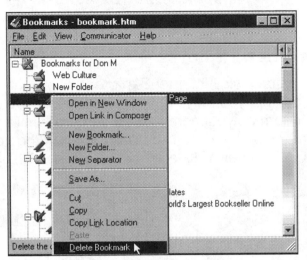

Print Web Pages

- You can print all information you find on the Internet.

To print a Web page:

✔ *Only displayed pages can be printed.*

1. Click the Print button on the Navigation toolbar.

   OR

   Click <u>F</u>ile, <u>P</u>rint.

2. In the Print dialog box that displays, select the desired print options and click OK.

- In most cases, the Web page will be printed in the format shown in the Web page display.

Microsoft Internet Explorer: 4

◆ Start Internet Explorer 4
◆ Internet Explorer Screen ◆ Exit Internet Explorer

Start Internet Explorer 4

- When you first install Internet Explorer and you are using the Active Desktop, you may see the message illustrated below when you turn on your computer. If you are familiar with Explorer 3, you may want to select 1 to learn the new features in Explorer 4. Select 2 to learn about Channels.

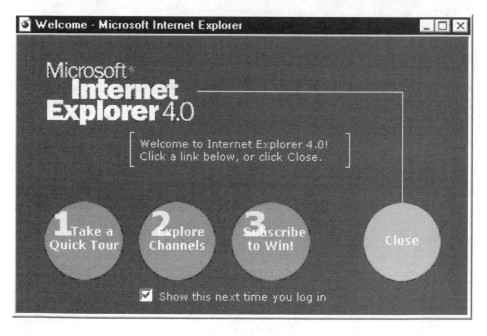

To start Internet Explorer:

- Click [Internet Explorer] on the Desktop.

  OR

  Click [e] on the Taskbar.

  OR

  Click the Start button [Start], then select Programs, Internet Explorer, and click Internet Explorer.

Internet Explorer Screen

- When you connect to the World Wide Web, the first screen that displays is called a home page. The home page is the first page of any World Wide Web site.

- You can change the first page that you see when you connect to Explorer.

To change the home page:

1. Click View, Internet Options.
2. Enter a new address in the Address text box.

   ✔ *The page that you see when you are connected may differ from the one illustrated below.*

3. Click [OK].

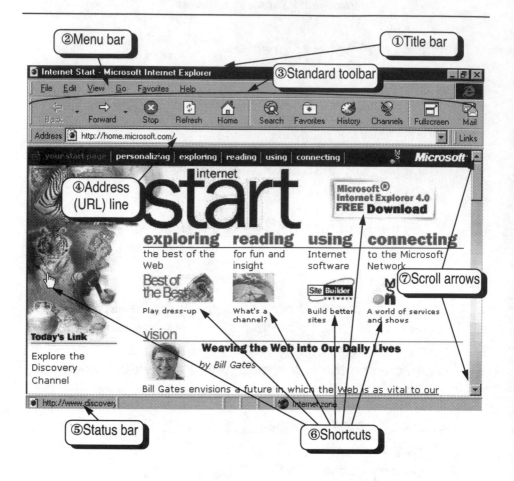

② Menu bar	① Title bar
③ Standard toolbar	
④ Address (URL) line	⑦ Scroll arrows
⑤ Status bar	⑥ Shortcuts

① **Title bar**   Displays the name of the program and the current Web page. You can minimize, restore, or close Explorer using the buttons on the right side of the Title bar.

Restore

Minimize   Close

② **Menu bar**   Displays menus currently available, which provide drop-down lists of commands for executing Internet Explorer tasks.

   The Internet Explorer button on the right side of the Menu bar rotates when action is occurring or information is being processed.

③ **Standard toolbar**   Displays frequently used commands.

④ **Address (URL) line**   Displays the address of the current page. You can click here, type a new address, press Enter, and go to a new location (if it's an active Web site). You can also start a search from this line.

The Links bar contains links to various Microsoft sites. Drag the split bar to the left or somewhere else on the screen to display current Links. You can add or delete links.

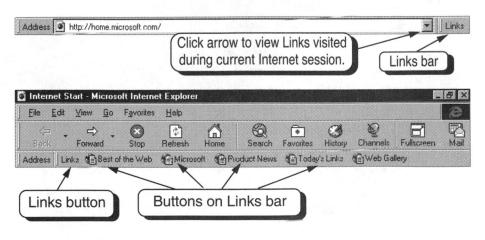

Click arrow to view Links visited during current Internet session.

Links bar

Links button

Buttons on Links bar

⑤ **Status bar**   Displays information about actions occurring on the page and the Security Level. Internet Security Properties lets you control content that is downloaded on to your computer.

⑥ **Shortcuts**   Click on shortcuts (also called hyperlinks) to move to other Web sites. Shortcuts are usually easy to recognize. They can be underlined text, text of different colors, "buttons" of various sizes and shapes, or graphics. You are pointing to a shortcut when the mouse pointer changes to a hand, and the full name of the Web site appears on the Status bar.

⑦ **Scroll arrows**   Scroll arrows are used to move the screen view, as in all Windows applications.

Exit Internet Explorer

■ Exiting Internet Explorer and disconnecting from your service provider are two separate steps. It is important to remember that if you close Internet Explorer (or any other browser), you must also disconnect (or hang up) from your service provider. If you don't disconnect, you'll continue incurring any applicable charges.

Microsoft Internet Explorer: 5

◆ **Standard Toolbar Buttons**
◆ **Open a Web Site from the Address Bar**

Standard Toolbar Buttons

- The Internet Explorer Standard toolbar displays frequently used commands. If the Standard toolbar is *not* visible when you start Explorer, open the View menu, select Toolbars, then select Standard Buttons.

Internet Explorer Toolbar and Functions

Moves back through pages previously displayed. Back is available only if you have moved around among Web pages in the current Explorer session.

Moves forward through pages previously displayed. Forward is available only if you have used the Back button.

Interrupts the opening of a page that is taking too long to display.

Reloads the current page.

Returns you to your home page. You can change your home page to open to any Web site or a blank page (View, Internet Options, General).

Allows you to select from a number of search services with a variety of options.

Displays the Web sites that you have stored or bookmarked using the Favorites menu.

Displays links to Web sites that you have visited in previous days and weeks. You can change the number of days that sites are stored in your History folder (View, Internet Options, General).

 Displays the list of current channels on the Explorer bar.

 Conceals Menu, titles, Status bar, and Address bar to maximize your screen for viewing a Web page. Click it again to restore your screen.

 Displays a drop-down menu with various Mail and News options.

Open a Web Site from the Address Bar

1. Click in the Address bar and start typing the address of the Web site you want to open.

2. If you have visited the site before, Internet Explorer will try to complete the address automatically. If it is the correct address, press Enter to go to it. If it is not the correct address, type over the suggested address that displayed on the line.

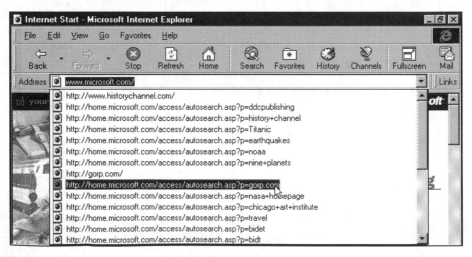

✔ *To turn off the AutoComplete feature, open the View menu, select Internet Options, and click the Advanced tab. Deselect Use AutoComplete in the Browsing area of the dialog box.*

Microsoft Internet Explorer: 6

◆ Open and Add to the Favorites Folder
◆ Open Web Sites from the Favorites Folder
◆ Create New Folders in the Favorites Folder
◆ AutoSearch from the Address Bar

Open and Add to the Favorites Folder

■ As you spend more time exploring Web sites, you will find sites that you want to visit frequently. You can store shortcuts to these sites in the Favorites folder.

To add a site to the Favorites folder:

1. Go to the desired Web site.
2. Open the Favorites menu or right-click anywhere on the page and select Add To Favorites.

   ✔ *The Add Favorite dialog box appears*

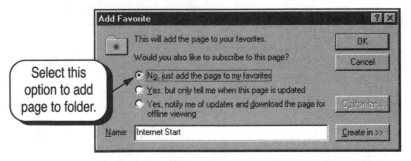

3. The name of the Page you have opened appears in the Name box. You may also choose to subscribe to a page. Subscribing to a page means you can schedule automatic updates to that site. Choose from the following options:

   ◆ No, just add the page to my favorites.

   ✔ *Choose this option to put a shortcut to the Web site in your Favorites folder.*

20

- ◆ <u>Y</u>es, but only tell me when this page is updated.

  ✔ *Explorer will alert you when an update to the site is available.*

- ◆ Yes, notify me of updates and <u>d</u>ownload the page for offline viewing

  ✔ *Explorer will automatically download and update to your computer.*

4. Click [OK] to add the Web address to the Favorites folder.

Open Web Sites from the Favorites Folder

- ■ Click the Favorites button [Favorites] on the Standard toolbar to open Web sites from the Favorites folder. The Explorer bar will open on the left side of the Browser window.

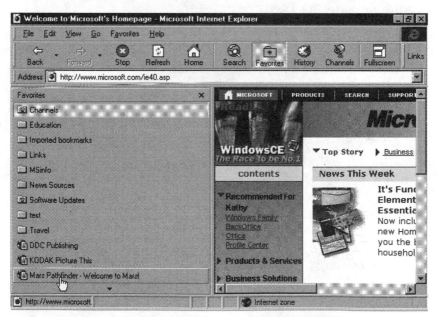

- ■ Click on an address or open a folder and select a site. Close the Explorer bar by clicking the Close button [X] or the

  Favorites button [Favorites] on the toolbar.

- You can also open the F<u>a</u>vorites menu and select a site from the list or from a folder.

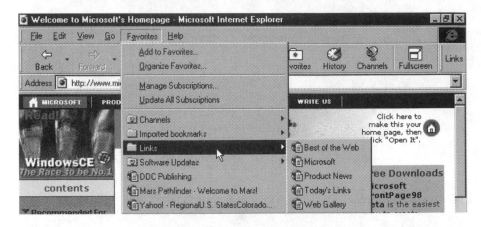

Create New Folders in the Favorites Folder

- You can create new folders before or after you have saved addresses in your Favorites folder.

To create a new folder:

1. Click F<u>a</u>vorites and select <u>O</u>rganize Favorites.
2. Click the Create New Folder button.
3. Type the name of the new folder and press Enter.

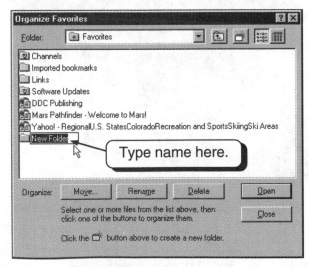

Type name here.

AutoSearch from the Address Bar

- In addition to displaying and entering addresses in the Address bar, you can use AutoSearch to perform a quick search directly from the Address bar.
- Click once in the Address bar and type *go, find,* or *?* and press the spacebar once. Enter the word or phrase you want to find and press Enter. For example, if you want to search for information about the year 2000, type *find the year 2000* on the Address bar and press Enter.

Address	find the year 2000

America Online: 7

About America Online

- America Online (AOL) is an all-purpose online service. Unlike Netscape Navigator or Microsoft Internet Explorer, AOL is not an Internet browser, yet you can browse the Internet using AOL navigation features.

- Unlike Internet browsers, AOL does not require a separate Internet Service Provider for Internet access, nor does it require a separate mail server connection to access e-mail from the AOL Mail Center.

Start America Online 4.0

1. Click the AOL icon on your desktop. This icon should display on your desktop after you install AOL.

   OR

   Click the Start button, Programs, America Online, America Online 4.0.

2. Make sure your screen name is displayed in the Select Screen Name box and type your password in the Enter Password box.

3. Click the Sign On button SIGN ON to connect to the AOL server.

The AOL Home Page, Menu, and Toolbar

- After you log on to America Online, you will see a series of screens. The final first screen you see is the AOL home page or start page. The AOL home page contains links to daily AOL featured areas and constant AOL areas such as *Channels* and *What's New*. You can also access your mailbox from the home page.

- The AOL menu displays currently available options. Click the menu item to display a drop-down list of links to AOL areas and basic filing, editing, and display options.

- The AOL toolbar contains buttons for AOL's most commonly used commands. Choosing a button activates the indicated task immediately.

	You have new mail if the flag on the mailbox is in the up position. Click to display your mailbox.
	Click to compose new mail messages.
	Click to read new, old, or sent mail; to set mail preferences; and to activate Flashsessions.
	Click to open the Print dialog box, where you can select from the standard print options.
	Click to access the Personal Filing Cabinet, where you can store e-mail messages, Newsgroup messages, and other files.
	Click to set AOL preferences, check personalized stock portfolios, read news and current events, set parental controls, passwords, and Buddy lists.
	Click this button to create links or shortcuts to your favorite Web sites or AOL areas.
	Click to connect to the Web, Internet directories, and Newsgroups.
	Click to access AOL's 21 channels, AOL areas, and Web site connections.
	Click to access the AOL Community Center, Chat Rooms, and meet the stars in the Live chat forum.
	Click to move to keywords or information entered on the URL line.
	Each AOL area has a keyword. Enter the keyword for immediate access to the desired AOL area.

AOL Help

■ AOL offers extensive Help so that you can learn to use AOL effectively.

■ To access Help, click Help and the help topic of choice from the menu.

Exit AOL

- To exit AOL, click the close window button ⊠ in the upper-right corner of the AOL screen.

  OR

  Click Sign Off, Sign Off on the menu bar.

  OR

  Click File, Exit.

America Online: 8

◆ Access the Internet from AOL
◆ Open a Wold Wide Web Site
◆ The AOL Browser Screen ◆ Stop a Load or Search

Access the Internet from AOL

- Click the Internet button [Internet] on the AOL main screen.

    OR

    Press Ctrl+K, type the word *internet* in the Keyword box and press Enter.

    ✔ *The Internet Connection window displays.*

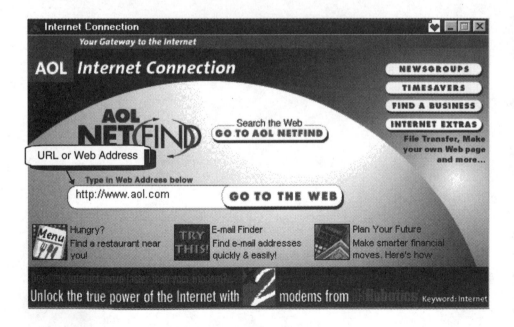

Open a World Wide Web Site

- If you know the Web address (URL), type it into the Type in Web Address below box and click the GO TO THE WEB button **GO TO THE WEB** or press Enter. If the Web address is correct, you will be connected to the Web site.
- If you wish to search the Internet, click the GO TO AOL NETFIND button **GO TO AOL NETFIND**.

The AOL Browser Screen

- Once you are connected to the Web, the screen below displays.

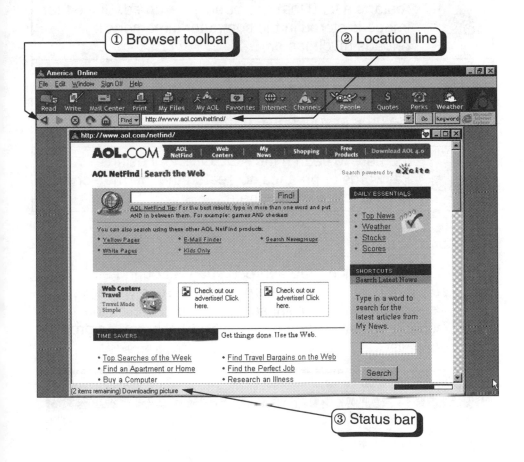

① Browser toolbar   ② Location line

③ Status bar

① Browser toolbar

- The AOL Browser toolbar will help you navigate through sites you visit on the Web. Buttons on the Browser toolbar also connect you to search and Internet preference areas.

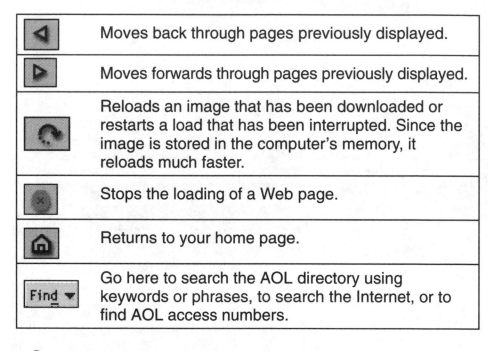

◁	Moves back through pages previously displayed.
▷	Moves forwards through pages previously displayed.
⟳	Reloads an image that has been downloaded or restarts a load that has been interrupted. Since the image is stored in the computer's memory, it reloads much faster.
⊗	Stops the loading of a Web page.
⌂	Returns to your home page.
Find ▼	Go here to search the AOL directory using keywords or phrases, to search the Internet, or to find AOL access numbers.

② Location line

- AOL stores each Web address you visit during each AOL session. If you wish to return to an address you have visited during the current session, you can click the location box arrow and click the address from the drop-down list.

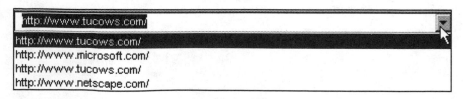

③ Status bar

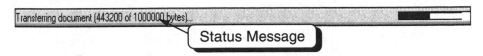

Transferring document (443200 of 1000000 bytes)...

Status Message

- The Status bar, located at the bottom of the screen, is a helpful indicator of the progress of the loading of a Web page. For example, if you are loading a Web site, you will see the byte size of the page, the percentage of the task completed, and the number of graphics and links yet to load. In many cases the time it will take to load the page will display.

Stop a Load or Search

■ Searching for information or loading a Web page can be time consuming, especially if the Web page has many graphic images, if a large number of people are trying to access the site at the same time, or if your modem and computer operate at slower speeds. If data is taking a long time to load, you may wish to stop a search or the loading of a page or large file.

- To stop a search or load click the Stop button on the Navigation toolbar.

- If you decide to continue the load after clicking the Stop button , click the Reload button .

America Online: 9

◆ Favorite Places ◆ Add Favorite Places
◆ View Favorite Places ◆ Delete Favorite Places
◆ AOL History List ◆ Save Web Pages
◆ Print Web Pages

Favorite Places

- A Favorite Place listing is a bookmark that you create containing the title, URL, and direct link to a Web page or AOL area that you may want to revisit.

- The AOL Favorite Place feature allows you to maintain a record of Web sites in your Favorite Places file so that you can return to them easily.

Add Favorite Places

- There are several ways to mark an AOL area or Web site and save it as a Favorite Place. Once the page is displayed:

  1. Click the Favorite Place icon 🖤 on the Web site or AOL area title bar.

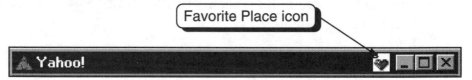

Favorite Place icon

🔺 Yahoo!

  2. Click on one of three options that display:

     Add to Favorites

     ✔ *The site will automatically be added to your Favorite Places list.*

     OR

     Insert in Instant Message

     ✔ *The site will automatically generate an Instant Message screen with a link to the site inserted.*

OR

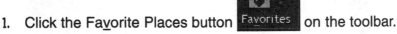

✔ *The site will automatically generate an e-mail composition screen with a link to the site inserted. Complete this as you would any e-mail message.*

OR

Display the Web page to add, right-click anywhere on the page and select Add to Favorites from the shortcut menu.

View Favorite Places

- You can view the Favorite Places file by clicking the Favorites button **Favorites** on the AOL toolbar and selecting Favorite Places. Click on any listing from the list to go directly to that page.

- The details of any Favorite Place listing can be viewed or modified by using the buttons on the Favorite Places screen.

Delete Favorite Places

- You may wish to delete a Favorite Place if a Web site no longer exists or an AOL area no longer interests you.

To delete a Favorite Place:

1. Click the Favorite Places button **Favorites** on the toolbar.
2. Click Favorite Places.
3. Click on the listing to delete.

4. Click the Delete button **Delete** from the Favorite Places screen.

   OR

   Right-click on the listing and select Delete from the pop-up menu.

   OR

Press the Delete key.

5. Click [Yes] to confirm the deletion.

AOL History List

- While you move back and forth within a Web site, AOL automatically records each page location. The History is only temporary and is deleted when you sign off. AOL areas are not recorded in the History list.

- To view the History list, click on the arrow at the end of the URL line. You can use History to jump back or forward to recently viewed pages by clicking on the page from the list.

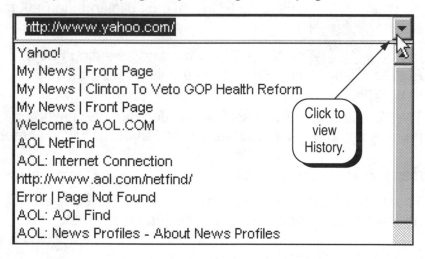

http://www.yahoo.com/

Yahoo!
My News | Front Page
My News | Clinton To Veto GOP Health Reform
My News | Front Page
Welcome to AOL.COM
AOL NetFind
AOL: Internet Connection
http://www.aol.com/netfind/
Error | Page Not Found
AOL: AOL Find
AOL: News Profiles - About News Profiles

Click to view History.

Save Web Pages

- When you find a Web page with information that you would like to keep for future reference or to review later offline, you can save it.

To save a Web page:

1. Click File, Save.

2. Type a filename in the File name box.

    ✔ When you save a Web page, often the current page name appears in the File name box. You can use this name or type a new one.

34

3. Choose the drive and folder in which to store the file from the Save in drop-down list.

4. Click Save.

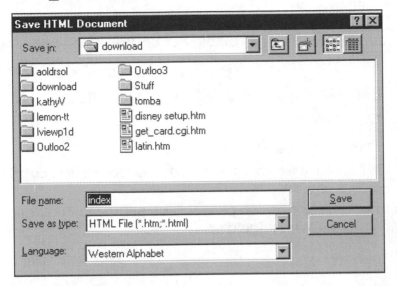

■ In most cases when you choose to save a Web page, AOL will automatically save it as an HTML file. Saving a page as an HTML file saves the original formatting and, when accessed, will display as you saw it on the Web.

■ You can also save a Web page as a plain text file, which saves only the page text without the formatting or images and placeholders. You might want to do this when saving a very large file, such as a literary work or multiple-page article. To save in plain text format, click the Save as type down arrow in the Save As dialog box and select plain text from the list.

■ You can view a saved Web page by clicking File, Open. In the Open a file dialog box, choose the location from the Look in drop-down list and double-click the file name.

Print Web Pages

- One of the many uses of the Internet is to find and print information.

To print a Web page, display it and do the following:

1. Click the Print button [Print] on the AOL toolbar.

   OR

   Click Print on the File menu.

2. In the Print dialog box that displays, select the desired print options and click OK.

- In most cases, the Web page will be printed in the format shown in the Web page display.

Search Engines: 10

Surfing vs. Searching

■ The Web has many thousands of locations, containing millions of pages of information. Unfortunately, the Internet has no uniform way of tracking and indexing everything.

■ Initially, it may seem easy to do research on the Web—you just connect to a relevant site and then start clicking on links to related sites. This random method of finding information on the Internet is called *surfing*. It may be interesting and fun, but there are drawbacks. Surfing is time consuming and the results are frequently inconsistent and incomplete. It can also be expensive if you are charged fees for connect time to your Internet Service Provider.

■ *Searching* is a more systematic and organized way of looking for information. You can connect to one of several search sites that use *search engines* to track, catalog, and index information on the Internet.

Search Sites

■ A *search site* builds its catalog using a search engine. A search engine is a software program that goes out on the Web, seeks Web sites, and catalogs them, usually by downloading their home pages.

■ Search sites are classified by the way they use search engines to gather Web site data. Below and on the following page is an explanation of how the major search services assemble and index information.

Search Engines

• Search engines are sometimes called *spiders* or *crawlers* because they crawl the Web.

- Search engines constantly visit sites on the Web to create catalogs of Web pages and keep them up to date.

- Major search engines include: AltaVista, HotBot, and Open Text.

Directories

- Search *directories* are created by people who catalog information by building hierarchical indexes. Directories may be better organized than search engine sites, but may not be as complete or up-to-date as search engines that constantly check for new material on the Internet.

- Yahoo!, the oldest search service on the World Wide Web, is the best example of an Internet search directory. Other major search directories are: Infoseek, Magellan, and Lycos.

Multi-Threaded Search Engines

- Another type of search engine, called a *multi-threaded* search engine, searches other Web search sites and gathers the results of these searches for your use.

- Because they search the catalogs of other search sites, multi-threaded search sites do not maintain their own catalogs. These search sites provide more search options than subject-and-keyword search sites, and they typically return more specific information with further precision. However, multi-threaded search sites are much slower to return search results than subject-and-keyword search sites.

- Multi-threaded search sites include SavvySearch and Internet Sleuth.

- If you are using Internet Explorer or Netscape Navigator, you can click on the Search button on the toolbar to access a number of search services.

Search Basics

- When you connect to a search site, the home page has a text box for typing the words you want to use in your search. These words are called a *text string*. The text string may be a single word or phrase.

- Once you have entered a text string, initiate the search by either pressing the Enter key or by clicking on the search button. This button may be called Search, Go Get It, Seek Now, Find, or something similar.

- For the best search results:

  - Always check for misspelled words and typing errors.

  - Use descriptive words and phrases.

  - Use synonyms and variations of words.

  - Find and follow the instructions that the search site suggests for constructing a good search.

  - Eliminate unnecessary words (the, a, an, etc.) from the search string. Concentrate on key words and phrases.

  - Test your search string on several different search sites. Search results from different sites can vary greatly.

  - Explore some of the sites that appear on your initial search and locate terms that would help you refine your search string.

Search Engines: 11

◆ Simple Searches ◆ Refine a Search ◆ Get Help

Simple Searches

- Searches can be simple or complex, depending on how you design the search string in the text box.

- A *simple search* uses a text string to search for matches in a search engine's catalog. A simple search is the broadest kind of search.

  - The text string may be specific, such as *Social Security*, *current stock quotes*, or *Macintosh computers*, or it may be general, such as *software*, *economy*, or *computer*.

  - The catalog search will return a list, typically quite large, of Web pages and URLs whose descriptions contain the text string you want to find. Frequently these searches will yield results with completely unrelated items.

- When you start a search, the Web site searches its catalog for occurrences of your text string. The results of the search are displayed in the window of your browser.

- Each search site has its own criteria for rating the matches of a catalog search and setting the order in which they are displayed.

- The catalog usually searches for matches of the text string in the URLs of Web sites. It also searches for key words, phrases, and meta-tags (key words that are part of the Web page, but are not displayed in a browser) in the cataloged Web pages.

- The information displayed on the results page will vary, depending on the search site and the search and display options you select. The most likely matches for your text string appear first in the results list, followed by other likely matches on successive pages.

✔ *There may be thousands of matches that contain your text string. The matches are displayed a page at a time. You can view the next page by clicking on the "next page" link provided at the bottom of each search results page.*

■ You can scan the displayed results to see if a site contains the information you want. Site names are clickable links. After visiting a site, you can return to the search site by clicking the Back button on your browser. You can then choose a different site to visit or perform another search.

Refine a Search

■ Suppose that you only want to view links that deal with Greek tragedies. Note, in the example below, the number of documents that were found when *Greek tragedies* was entered in this search. Since the search string didn't include a special *operator* to tell the search engine to look for sites that contain both Greek *and* tragedies, the results display sites that contain Greek *or* tragedies in addition to sites that contain Greek *and* tragedies.

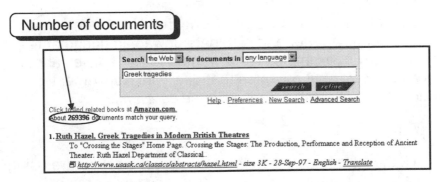

■ To reduce the number of documents in this search, use operators—words or symbols that modify the text string instead of being part of it. Enter *Greek,* space once, then enter a plus sign (+) and the word *tragedies* (Greek +tragedies) then click Search. This tells AltaVista to look for articles that contain Greek *and* tragedies in the documents. Note the results that display when the plus is added to the search.

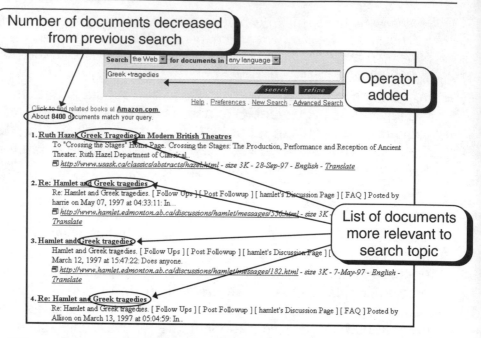

Number of documents decreased from previous search

Search the Web ▼ for documents in any language ▼

Greek +tragedies

search   refine

Operator added

Help . Preferences . New Search . Advanced Search

Click to find related books at **Amazon.com.**

About **8400** documents match your query.

1. **Ruth Hazel Greek Tragedies in Modern British Theatres**
   To "Crossing the Stages" Home Page. Crossing the Stages: The Production, Performance and Reception of Ancient Theater. Ruth Hazel Department of Classical.
   http://www.usask.ca/classics/abstracts/hazel.html - size 3K - 28-Sep-97 - English - *Translate*

2. **Re: Hamlet and Greek tragedies**
   Re: Hamlet and Greek tragedies. [Follow Ups] [Post Followup] [hamlet's Discussion Page] [FAQ] Posted by harrie on May 07, 1997 at 04:33:11: In...
   http://www.hamlet.edmonton.ab.ca/discussions/hamlet/messages/556.html - size 3K - *Translate*

List of documents more relevant to search topic

3. **Hamlet and Greek tragedies**
   Hamlet and Greek tragedies. [Follow Ups] [Post Followup] [hamlet's Discussion Page] [March 12, 1997 at 15:47:22: Does anyone.
   http://www.hamlet.edmonton.ab.ca/discussions/hamlet/messages/182.html - size 3K - 7-May-97 - English - *Translate*

4. **Re: Hamlet and Greek tragedies**
   Re: Hamlet and Greek tragedies. [Follow Ups] [Post Followup] [hamlet's Discussion Page] [FAQ] Posted by Allison on March 13, 1997 at 05:04:59: In...

- The number of results is dramatically reduced, and the documents displayed display information that is more closely related to the topic, *Greek tragedies.*

- You can also *exclude* words by using the minus sign (-) to refine a search further and eliminate unwanted documents in the results. For example, if you wanted to find articles about Greek tragedies but not ones that deal with Hamlet, enter a search string like this: *Greek +tragedies -Hamlet.*

Get Help

- Check the Help features on the search tool that you are using to see what operators are available. Since there are no standards governing the use of operators, search sites can develop their own.

Search Engines: 12

◆ AltaVista ◆ Yahoo! ◆ excite

- Web searches can be frustrating. There are, however, a few basic tips that will almost always help you find what you want.

- Following are search tips for three of the most popular search sites. Each search site is different but some search techniques are universal.

AltaVista

http://altavista.digital.com/

- Enter your text string in the Search box. Make sure all words are spelled correctly.

- You may modify your search string with operators to narrow the search results. This will help you find more information specifically relevant to your search.

  - To modify your search string, put a (+) in front of the words that *must* be in your results and a (–) in front of the words that must *not* be in your results.

43

- Always use lowercase letters when searching the Web using AltaVista unless you are using proper nouns.

- You can also enter exact phrases into the search text box. If you are looking for pages that contain an exact phrase, enclose the phrase in the Search box with quotation marks.

- Search Usenets (Newsgroups) to read public opinion and postings on thousands of topics.

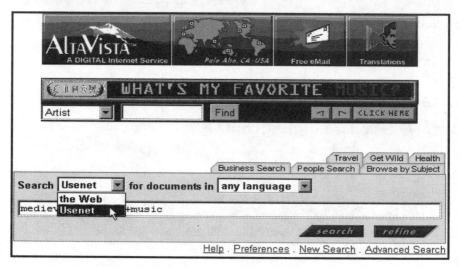

- Go to the AltaVista search areas found at the top of the search box to search a collection of Web pages and sites on everything from Travel to People.

- Click on AltaVista *Help* to get more information on searches.

Yahoo!

http://www.Yahoo.com

- Yahoo! searches for information in the four databases contained in its search catalog:

  - **Yahoo! Categories:**
    Web pages organized under different categories such as History, Economy, and Entertainment.

  - **Yahoo! Web Sites:**
    A list of Web page links that are relevant to your search.

  - **Yahoo!'s Net Events & Chat:**
    A list of events and live chats on the Web that are relevant based on words in your search string.

  - **Most Recent News Articles:**
    A database of over 300 online publications for articles that contain your keywords.

- Enter the keywords of your search in the search box. Make sure the words are spelled correctly.

- Be as specific as possible when entering keywords into the search box.

- Use a **(+)** in front of any keyword that must appear in the document and a **(-)** in front of words that should not.

- Yahoo! provides search syntax options to help you modify your search.

- To display search syntax options, click the *options* link next to the Search button from the home page. The following dialog box displays:

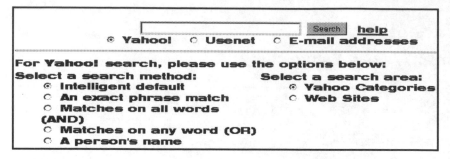

- You can also do a search by document title and URL.

- Place a *t:* in front of one or more keywords to yield Web pages with the keywords in the title of the page.

- Place a *u:* in front of keywords to yield returns with the keyword in the URL. Your search should return pages dedicated to the subject of your keywords.

- Yahoo! has specialized search areas. Click on any of the links on the Yahoo! home page to search for anything from stock quote information to buying a pet or an automobile. These links contain extensive information.

excite

http://www.excite.com/

- excite searches the Web by concept using Intelligent Concept Extraction (ICE) to find the relationships between words and ideas.

- Enter concepts and ideas rather than keywords into the search box.

- You can further modify your search by adding words supplied by excite based on the keywords or phrase you've entered.

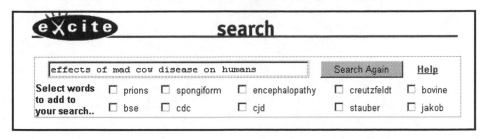

- Modify the words in your search phrase by using the (+) and (−) signs.
- Click *Help* to read more on excite search.
- You can activate a Power Search. This search uses the excite Search Wizard to help focus your search.
- Click the *Power Search* link located to the left of the search box on the excite home page. Enter the keywords or idea into the search box, as shown below.

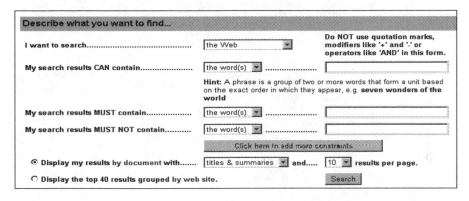

SHOP THE WEB

Getting Started

Internet Shopping

- The Internet provides vast opportunities for shopping and purchasing. But if you're shopping online, your main objective is probably to save time, energy, and money. Although it can be fun, you don't want to waste a lot of time surfing the Internet.

- From antique vases to running shoes to automobiles— whatever it is you're seeking, you're bound to find it on the Internet. Just like shopping in the "real world," however, the trick to bargain shopping on the Web lies not in your ability to find what you want fast, but in your ability to get the best product at the best price from a reputable source.

Principles of Bargain Shopping

- The Web Resource section of this book is designed to guide you through the following four principles of online bargain shopping:

  1. Browse before you buy.

  2. Visit specialty shops.

  3. Shop comparison prices.

  4. Make safe, secure purchases.

The Process

- If you do not know the exact product name and model of the item you want, or if you just want to browse the limitless shopping opportunities available or the Internet, your best bet is to start at a general site, directory, megasite, or Internet mall. These sites are usually organized by different categories, such as Clothing, Grocery, Computers, Flowers, etc.

- Each category links you to merchandisers who sell related products and services. For example, if you want to purchase a sleeping bag, you would most likely click on a Sports and Leisure (or similar) category within one of these sites. You would then be linked to a site that contains links to merchandisers who sell sleeping bags.

- Once you have located the exact item you want to purchase, hold tight. Don't make your final purchase just yet. Our Comparison Shopping section will walk you through obtaining the best possible price for the item of your choice.

Welcome to the Mall!

◆ Mall Basics ◆ America Online
◆ Microsoft Network ◆ Choice Mall ◆ Imall.com
◆ virtualemporium ◆ 21st Century Plaza
◆ 123Commerce.com

Mall Basics

- If you want to find a product or service on the Web fast but don't know where to look, the best place to start is at a directory, general site, or Internet mall.

- Basically, all three of these types of Web sites are similar in that they organize various shopping sites on the Web so that you don't waste excess time randomly searching.

Directories

- A directory Web site looks just like a directory you might find in a "real world" mall. You'll find category listings such as Clothing, House and Garden, Sports and Leisure, Grocery, etc. Within each category, the directory lists links to related merchandisers' Web sites.

General Sites

- Another easy way to start your shopping venture is by using a general site. A general site is a Web site that primarily offers other services such as Internet access and banking. Often, these sites also contain direct links to merchandisers as well as directories that categorize shopping opportunities on the Web.

- In their battle to stay ahead of the competition, general sites such as America Online and Microsoft Network are now providing gateways to excellent shopping areas in addition to their regular online services. These readily available resources eliminate the need to surf the sometimes confusing and tangled Web.

Internet Malls

- Like general sites and directories, Internet malls consist of specialized categories for various services and goods. Unlike general sites and directories, Internet malls are not part of a larger online service. They function the same way that directories do, and organize Web site links by category.

- When you shop at a general site, directory site, or Internet Mall, you'll make separate purchases at each online store you visit. Your purchases are made from the actual merchandiser and not the primary site that linked you to the store. After you are through browsing or making purchases in one store, you can use your browser's Back button to return to the main shopping site and then select another store to visit.

- Keep in mind that the shopping links you find at directories, general sites, and Internet Malls are companies who have chosen to advertise with that particular Web site. Therefore, these sites do not always offer you the widest range of online options or rock-bottom prices.

- You'll find that the sites listed in this topic vary slightly in their organization and structure, but their functions are generally the same.

America Online

http://www.aol.com

The leading commercial online service provides direct links to merchandisers, a comprehensive Shop by Category directory, a powerful search engine, and AOL Yellow Pages for locating merchants in a specified area.

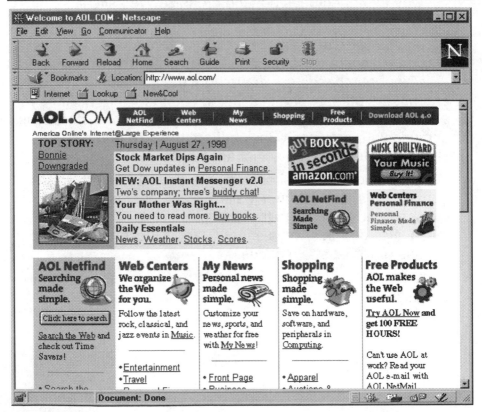

- The AOL Web site isn't just for Internet newcomers and home Web surfers. In addition to the direct link to featured products and online merchandisers, it provides a good jumping-off point for practical shopping.

- The *Shopping* link connects you to AOL's Shop by Category Web site, a simple, well-organized directory that contains links to several high-quality merchants.

- If you don't find what you're looking for online with the AOL categories, give the AOL Yellow Pages a try. This feature allows you to search for a product in a particular city and state. AOL then generates a list of applicable merchandisers for the specified area.

- Click the *Web Centers* link to access links to bargain travel, groceries, entertainment, and more.

- The *Time Savers* link helps you plan common day-to-day tasks such as reserving airline tickets, renting a video, or ordering take-out.

- Another way to search for products or services via the AOL Web site is to use NetFind, AOL's powerful search engine. Type the specific item you wish to find and your search results should contain links to merchants selling the item you specified. Your results may also contain online reviews, informational sites, or sites with little relevance. Be sure to scan your list carefully in order to avoid wasting time wandering through inapplicable sites.

Microsoft Network

http://www.msn.plaza.com

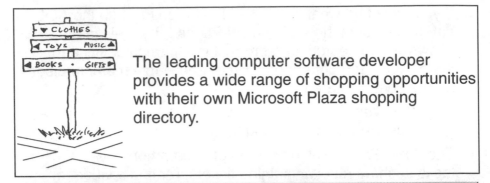

The leading computer software developer provides a wide range of shopping opportunities with their own Microsoft Plaza shopping directory.

- The Microsoft Plaza directory page offers a surplus of purchasing and bargain hunting opportunities. The directory is broken into several sections, each featuring applicable merchandisers.

- The Plaza Merchants section contains categories representing everything from Bargains to Sports to Home and Garden. Each category lists an array of links to popular merchants and discount stores.

- The Plaza Promotions section offers frequently updated sales and special promotions. Offers may change on a minute-to-minute basis, so be sure to act quickly if something catches your eye.

- The Plaza Specials section provides links to merchandisers who can assist you with shipping, packaging, or gift wrapping your purchases. Check out the *More $ Savings Specials* link, which allows you to sign up for an e-mail list that will alert you when special bargains, sales, and promotions become available.

- The Gift Reminder feature allows you to plug in birthday and anniversary dates for all the important people in your life. It will then send you an e-mail reminder—in advance—so that you'll be sure not to forget the event.

Choice Mall

http://www.choicemall.com

With more than 1400 stores to shop, Choice Mall bills itself as the Internet's primary global marketplace.

- Find daily bargains and savings with featured brand-name items on the Choice Mall home page. Or, click the *Hot Deals* link to find wholesale-priced items, coupons, free offers, and other specials. Also from the home page, click the *Contests* link for a chance to win a $1,000 shopping spree.

- In addition to searching by product category, you can find specific items or services quickly with Choice Mall's search feature.

- Along with the regular features you would expect to find at a huge mall, you'll also find links to business and financial services, real estate listings, medical and health sites, educational and professional services, and discount travel sites.

- Click the *Regions* link on the home page to find information on shopping, culture, weather, schools, and maps for areas near you or places you plan to visit.

iMALL.com

http://www.imall.com/

One of the newest megamall sites on the Web, iMALL is striving to become the premier gateway to Internet shopping.

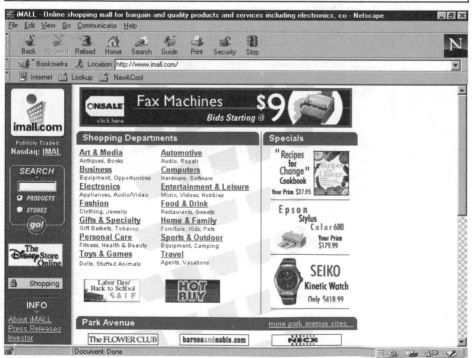

- Search the humongous iMALL inventory of shops and products by keyword or category. iMALL's search feature will find specific products for you and list choices from a variety of vendors. Or, link directly to hundreds of boutiques, specialty stores, discount outlets, and premium shopping sites.

- If you're looking for upscale merchants, you'll find links to stores like FAO Schwartz, the Disney Store Online, and Gourmet Market in the Park Avenue department.

- Look on the home page for daily specials on products and services, newly added online merchants, and quick links to sales and hot buys. The Features department includes news on limited deals, information on where you can save 15-30% on brand-name products, links to international shopping, and classifieds that you can search for deals, sales, and other opportunities.

- You can register to become a member of *CLUB iMALL* for preferred services. You will also be notified of any new additions to the mall or special sales in areas that you specify.

- All iMALL vendors ensure safe and secure shopping. Furthermore, iMALL offers refunds on purchases in the event of proven fraudulent credit card usage.

virtualemporium

http://virtualemporium.com

This attractive site offers easy access to all of your favorite major stores and merchants.

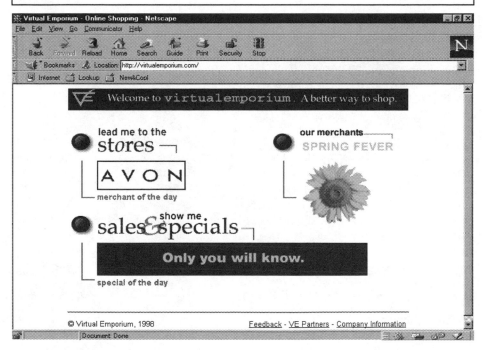

- Go to the virtualemporium for quick links to JCPenny, Macy's, Wal-Mart, Eddie Bauer, Spiegel, and Avon, to name only a few. You can also find links to major airlines, car dealerships and rental agencies, banks, real estate, and professional services.

- Click the *Sales & Specials* link for daily discounts and exclusive online offers on thousand of goods in all virtualemporium shopping departments. Also check out the *Seasonal* link for season-specific deals that you can enjoy all year round.

21st Century Plaza

http://21stcenturyplaza.com/

Rated among the top 25 internet malls by *PC Computing,* 21st Century Plaza offers the highest quality service and secure shopping to its online customers.

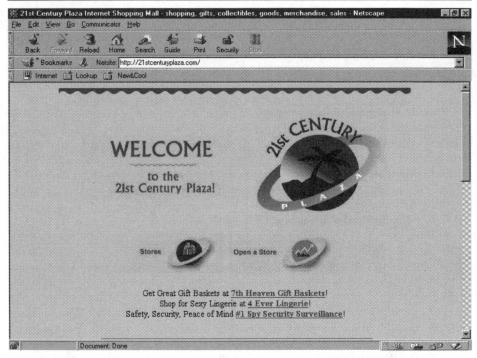

- Navigation through the Plaza is easy—each site you link to maintains a 21st Century Plaza logo for quick links to the home page, other plaza areas, and help. All merchants offer 20% off retail prices in addition to special deals, discounts, and sales.

- If you can't find what you're looking for, contact customer service—they'll search the Internet for you and see if they can meet your needs.

123Commerce.com

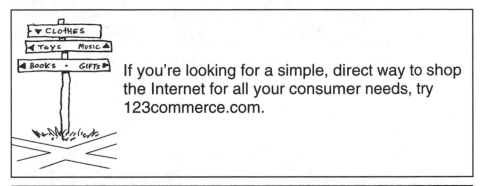

If you're looking for a simple, direct way to shop the Internet for all your consumer needs, try 123commerce.com.

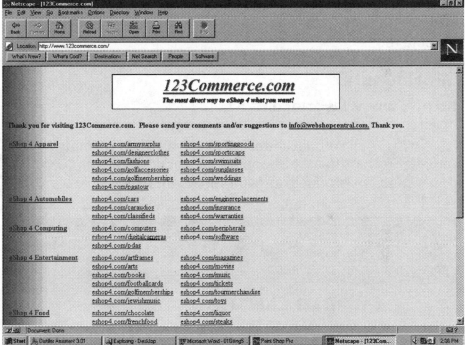

- This site offers links to major shopping sites without the glitz and glamour of other Internet Malls and directories. Come here for shopping resources—and lots of them.

- 123Commerce.com is organized much like an FTP directory, with just a simple list of "eShop4" links to numerous sites from apparel, automobiles, computing, and entertainment, to food, specialty gifts, tools, and travel.

Megasites

◆ 1WorldCenter ◆ The Internet Mall
◆ BuySafe.com ◆ NetMarket

Megasites are individual Web sites that provide one-stop shopping for a multitude of products and services. One virtual shopping cart and one trip to the online cash register is all you'll need to shop at a megasite. Much like bargain warehouse stores in the "real world," megasites offer you the opportunity to buy products and services from several manufacturers under one discount roof.

1WorldCenter

http://www.1worldcenter.com/

1WorldCenter bills itself as "The Ultimate Internet Shopping Location" with over 40,000 products in 140 brand name stores.

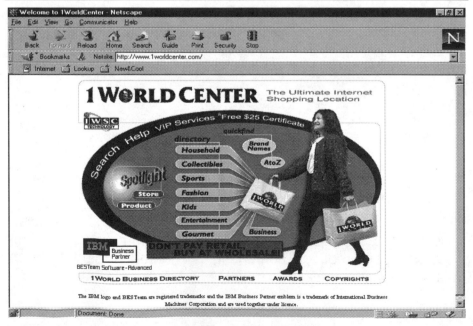

- Whatever your shopping needs, you will likely meet them here. 1WorldCenter will even get you started with a free $25 gift certificate toward any of the participating merchants at this site. You can register as a VIP member and be eligible for special services, including personal mailing lists, reminders, personal shoppers, bridal and baby registry, and free electronic greeting and thank you cards.

- From the home page, click on a category link, such as *Household, Entertainment, Kids, Fashion, Collectibles, Gourmet, Sports,* or *Business.* You will then see a list of participating stores you can browse or shop. Be sure to check out the monthly specials and wholesale offers, too.

- If you are looking for brand names, use the search feature to find what you want immediately. Click the *Search A to Z Brands* link to find merchandise by Cuisinart, Krups, Lenox Lorris, Oneida, Montblanc, Swiss Army, Wilson, Fuji, and much more.

- Shopping is guaranteed 100% secure at this Better Business Bureau member site, which has been rated a Certified Safe Shopping Site by The Public Eye. The Public Eye is a watchdog organization for certified safe shopping sites. 1WorldCenter also carries 100% unconditional guarantees on all orders placed through the site and honors all manufacture warranties.

The Internet Mall

http://www.internetmall.com

This award-winning megasite is a combination directory and ShopNow superstores site. With links to over 25,000 stores, you can find hundreds of brand-name products at very reasonable prices.

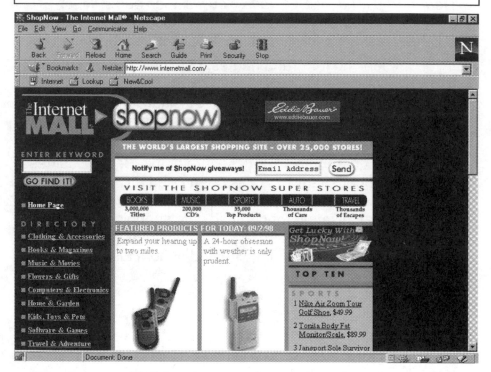

- The Internet Mall has been a pioneer in online shopping since 1994, providing e-shoppers with one central location totally dedicated to the best (and most!) shopping sites on the Web. All Merchants listed with the Internet Mall have access to secure electronic commerce service.

- Find instant bargains and the top ten best deals of the day listed on the home page. Click any of the ShopNow links to access easy-to-find deals and millions of choices in books, music, sports, autos, and travel adventures.

- Be sure to click the *Help* link on the home page to find out about giveaways, contests, promotions, special sales and rebate items, tracking your shipping order, and customer service options.

BuySafe.com

http://buysafe.com

 The Buysafe.com shopping experience is a blend of Internet boutique service and megastore inventory.

- From the BuySafe.com home page, you can click various shopping categories to see a larger selection of online stores. As you browse through all the shops, the Buysafe.com navigation bar remains at the bottom of your screen. Use the navigation bar to go to another store instantly, add to your order, view items in your shopping cart, and get 24/7 free customer assistance.

- Although BuySafe.com doesn't feature as many stores as some of the other Internet malls and megasites, the partnered stores have been chosen for the integrity and quality of their products. Shop at many stores and check out at one register through a secure server.

- BuySafe stands behind its merchants and their inventory and offers free shipping and money-back guarantees in the event of fraudulent purchases. Click *Help* for more details. If you plan on becoming a frequent shopper, you can set up a personal secure account for faster and easier service.

NetMarket

http://www.netmarket.com

This megasite has more than 800,000 brand name products for you to browse and buy at wholesale prices.

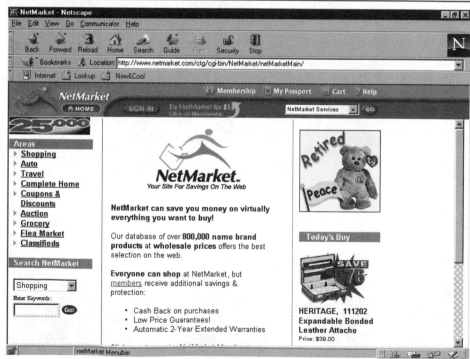

- At NetMarket, you can shop tons of categories for home, office, garden, travel, and leisure. NetMarket also has a new and used car buying service, trip routing, car care, and accessories.

- Find additional savings with coupons and discounts, live online auctions, grocery items, flea markets, and classifieds.

- To take complete advantage of this one-stop-shopping mall, it pays to register. For a negligible fee, NetMarket members get additional discounts and privileges, including incredible savings on vacation packages and extended warrantees on all purchases. Members also get NetMarket Cash Back on purchases, free gifts, privileged bids in auctions, and members-only specials.

- View the contents of your shopping cart and add or delete items at any time.

Catalog Sites

◆ The Catalog Site ◆ Catalog Mart
◆ Catalog World ◆ CatalogSavings
◆ Other Sites

Whether you're a self-proclaimed aficionado of cooking, fishing, biking, gardening, automobiles, chocolate, lingerie, or hi-tech gadgets, you know that catalogs often offer the best in niche-market shopping. Now you can find all your favorite catalogs online and discover new ones. The advantages of catalog shopping online often adds up to additional discounts, limited offers, and VIP features that aren't always available in the printed catalogs.

The Catalog Site

http://www.catalogsite.com

The ultimate megasite for all catalogs, The Catalog Site offers hundreds of free catalogs for you to explore, compare, and shop from.

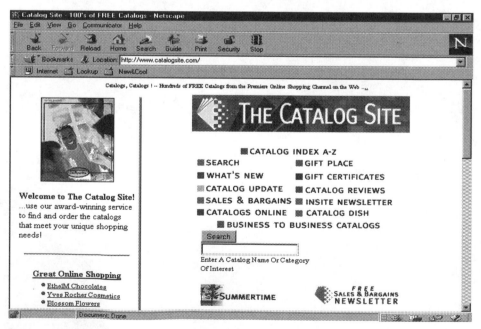

- Whether you're looking for catalogs by name or by subject, make The Catalog Site your first online stop. In addition to the hundreds of catalogs organized by subject, you'll find excellent search features, gift certificates, bargains, and reviews. Have catalogs sent directly to your home, or shop immediately at the catalog online sites.

- Check this award-winning site frequently for shopper-savvy features, such as "Item of the Day" special offers, Catalog Dish articles, select sales, and bargains. You can also sign up with the MyPoint Program and earn free points redeemable for travel, merchandise, and entertainment.

- In addition to catalogs, you can browse hundreds of special interest magazines and order yearly subscriptions directly from the site. The Catalog Site offers gift certificates and gift registry for a variety of specialty catalog merchants.

- Have the free *Catalog Insite* newsletter e-mailed to you monthly for the latest scoop about cool new companies and the best bargains and sales on the Internet.

Catalog Mart

http://catalog.savvy.com

Find virtually any catalog available in the US and have it shipped to you at no charge.

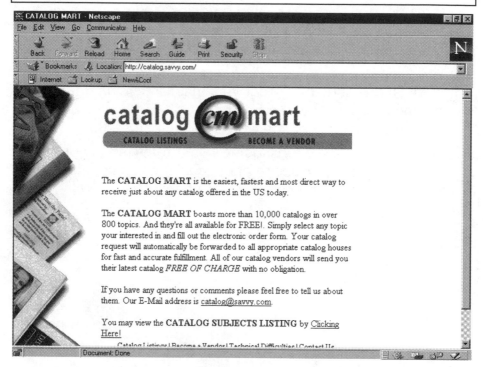

- Catalog Mart is one of the Web's most comprehensive catalog listing sites with more than 10,000 catalogs in over 800 special interest topics. Have catalogs sent directly to you free of charge and free of obligation, or access catalog sites to order online.

- The beauty of this site is its simplicity. From the home page, click *Catalog Listings* to jump directly to the catalog request page. Enter your e-mail and mailing address information, then select from an alphabetical listing of thousands of special interests. When you find what you're looking for, simply click to check your selections, and then submit your query.

- Catalog Mart will send your order directly to the selected vendors, who in turn will ship you their latest catalog. If you experience technical problems or if your browser doesn't support forms, you can contact the customer service department who will help you fill your order.

- Catalog Mart is truly for the serious shopper, and requests that you only order catalogs from which you expect to buy products, so that this service can remain free of charge to the public.

Catalog World

http://www.catalogworld.com

 Catalog lovers, order hundreds upon hundreds of the best catalogs for free or link directly to your favorite online catalog sites.

- You may order from Catalog World online or via telephone. Additionally, more than 7,000 catalogs are listed with all phone, fax, and address information, so that you may contact them directly.

- You only need to register with Catalog World once for quick processing. Simply click the *request* button next to the catalog of your choice, and your information is processed instantly. You don't need to go through any final checkouts. If you are a returning visitor, simply log on with your user name and password, and request away!

- Most catalogs take two to four weeks to arrive. If you feel that you did not receive a catalog that you should have, send an e-mail to Catalog World customer service, and they'll follow up on your request for you.

CatalogSavings

http://catalog.catalogsavings.com/

 Joan and Jackie are hosts of this site that specializes in offering you the world's best catalogs and amazing money-saving offers with exclusive catalog savings certificates.

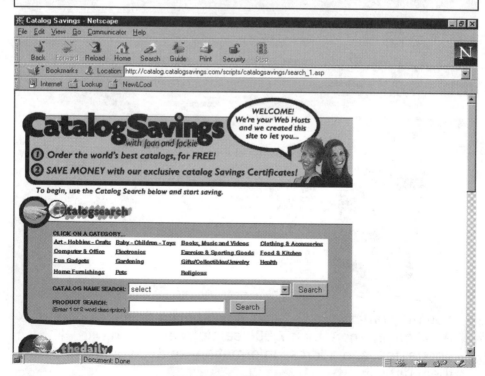

- Search the CatalogSavings inventory by catalog name or by product. Read detailed catalog profiles for complete descriptions of what they offer. For each catalog you order, you'll also get a Savings Certificate, which you can print out and redeem. You can also link directly to sites and order online.

- Be sure to explore all the areas on the home page for daily discount scoops, gift certificates, and special product drawings. Joan and Jackie are continually adding new catalogs, making this site worth checking out for frequent bargain finds.

Other Sites

CatalogFinder™
http://www.catalogfinder.com

- Order from more than 15,000 catalogs from all over the world, view catalog Web sites, or shop directly from the catalog online sites. Join the Members Only Shopping club for customized shopping services. This is an excellent resource for foreign language and international catalogs.

SkyMall
http://www.skymall.com

- If you're one of the 375 million Americans who fly every year, then you're surely familiar with SkyMall, the most popular in-flight catalog. SkyMall features premium merchandise from numerous specialty retailers and other major catalog companies. Now, you don't have to wait until the next time you board an airplane to see what's new in the SkyMall catalog.

- Register as a preferred customer and get such perks as special offers, discounts, promotions, and VIP customer service.

Auction Sites

◆ Internet Auction List ◆ eBay ◆ Yahoo! Auctions
◆ Other Sites

Whether you're a serious collector or savvy bargain hunter, if you're eager to get what you want at incredibly low prices, consider going to an online auction. Bid against other e-shoppers for electronic products, real estate, cars, government surplus items, antiques, and hard-to-find values—all at insanely cheap prices.

Internet Auction List

http://www.internetauctionlist.com

Come to this comprehensive site for your one-stop resource of hundreds upon hundreds of Internet auction sites.

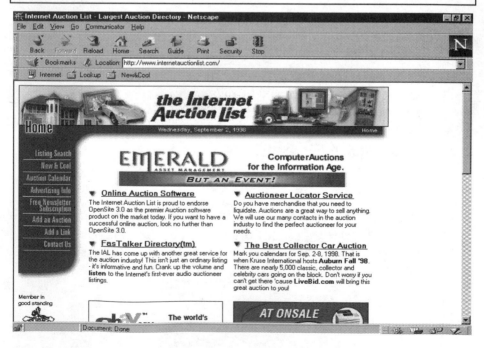

- This massive, well organized site is a great place to start if you're looking to break into the auction circuit. A member of the National Auctioneers Association, Internet Auction List is the largest resource for auction company sites on the Internet.

- Click a specialty item in the category list on the home page to link to upcoming related auctions as well as dozens of category-specific auction sites on the Web. You can read short descriptions of each site for easier navigation.

- If you attend auctions regularly, subscribe to the free IAL newsletter for the latest information on upcoming auctions and events. Do you have merchandise you'd like to sell? IAL offers an auctioneer locator service to find the perfect match for your needs.

eBay™

http://www.ebay.com/

 One of the hottest auction sites on the Web, (140,000,000 hits per week!) eBay has hundreds of thousands of items available for sale.

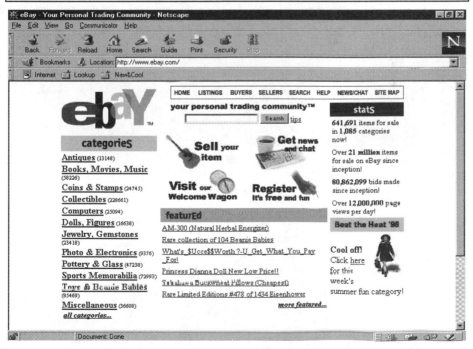

- This friendly site treats all its buyers and sellers as part of a community. The site's popularity has grown to make eBay the largest person-to-person trading area on the Internet.

- Newcomers start your eBay journey at the *Welcome Wagon* to learn how the site is set up to serve the trading community. Or, if you'd like a detailed tour, take the New User Tutorial.

- Once you're ready to explore your bidding or selling options, you need to register. Then, you can explore all the great stuff eBay has in its database, and bid for the items of your choice.

- Click on any of the category links and begin searching for that special item. Once you have found it, you can bid. If your bid is a winner, the only cost to you is the bid amount, which you pay directly to the seller.

- Bidding is easy, as eBay bids on your behalf. You tell them the maximum amount you are willing to bid, and they will continue to bid as necessary until someone outbids your maximum amount. Your maximum amount is kept confidential and, with luck, may never be reached.

- eBay also has excellent bulletin boards, chat rooms, and newsgroups. If you read through all the FAQs and still have questions, get live 24-hour support and information. Also be sure to check for great links to new features, buyer and seller services, and hot news.

Yahoo! Auctions

http://auctions.yahoo.com/

One of the Web's leading search directories now has a comprehensive auction site.

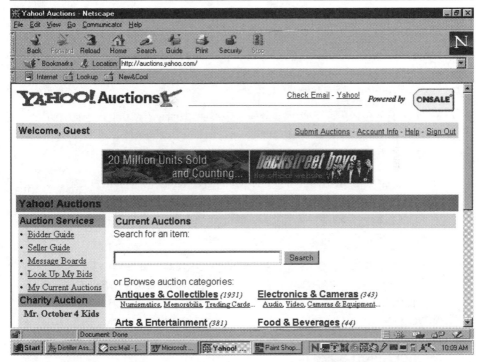

- On the home page, you can browse through numerous auction categories, including Antiques & Collectibles, Computers, Sports & Recreation, Toys & Games, and other goods. Each category lists the number of currently available items—ranging from hundreds to thousands of listings. Or, for a quick peek at all the goods up for auction, click the *Full Category Index* link. To bid on an item, you must register at the site and get a user name and password.

- Once you find an item you like, you can place a bid simply by entering your desired bidding amount. You can find out within seconds if your bid is currently winning. Yahoo! will notify you by e-mail if you are outbid, in which case you may choose to place a higher bid. Yahoo! then notifies winners via e-mail when the auction closes. Inventory changes frequently, so this is a site you'll want to check often.

- Yahoo! Auctions also has Message Boards where you can read news on upcoming hot items, learn bidding strategies, find out about swap meets and conventions, and get answers to questions you may have about auction etiquette and pricing.

Other Sites

DealDeal

http://www.dealdeal.com

- If you consider yourself a savvy shopper, you can make out with some of the best auction deals on the Internet at this site.

- Although primarily known for hardware, software, and electronic goods, you can find hard-to-beat deals on sporting goods, mountain bikes, kitchen and home items, and much more.

- Register to become a member and get $5 worth of free DealBucks toward any auction purchase. DealDeal will monitor your bids, e-mail you with status changes, notify you when you win, and establish a DealBucks account for you. All transactions are guaranteed secure through encryption software.

United States Treasury Auctions

http://www.ustreas.gov/auctions/

- If you're in the market for cheap property, vehicles, jewelry, artwork, equipment, and other consumer goods, take a look and see what Uncle Sam is selling.

- The U.S. Treasury Department regularly auctions off real estate and goods that have been unclaimed in the mail, or confiscated by Customs, the IRS, Criminal Investigations Division, the U.S. Secret Service, and the Bureau of Alcohol, Tobacco, and Firearms.

Price Comparison Search Sites

◆ **Bottom Dollar** ◆ **Jango!**
◆ **Other Sites**

Once you've narrowed your shopping search down to the product and model name (or number) you want to buy, simply plug the information into the search boxes at any price comparison search site. The results will show a list of merchandisers who are currently selling the item. You can then sort the information by price to determine who is offering the best deal.

Bottom Dollar

http://www.bottomdollar.com/

One of the easiest price comparison search sites on the Web, Bottom Dollar lets you select a category and begin your search right from its home page.

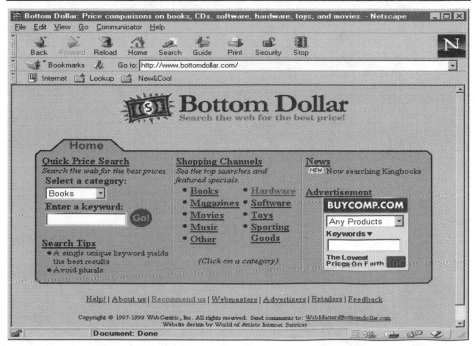

- The Bottom Dollar price comparison search site is great for finding low prices fast. Simply select a category (or Shopping Channel), type a keyword—usually a specific product name—and press Go! Within seconds you'll get a list of online merchants who are selling the item.

- If you don't know what category to select for the item you want, select the *Other* category. This will produce results from all applicable categories. For example, if you select the *Books* category and search on the keyword *airplanes*, the results will consist of books about airplanes. However, if you wish to broaden your airplane search to include magazines, toys, software, etc., you must select the *Other* category.

Jango

http://www.jango.com

Use this powerful search engine, which is part of the Excite search site, to match prices from countless merchandisers.

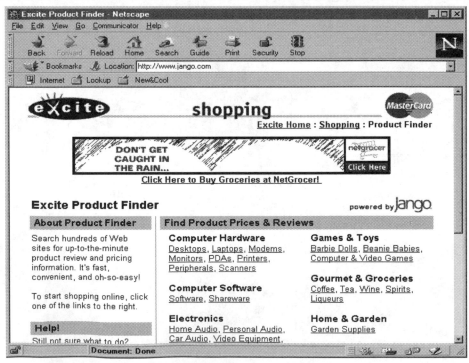

- Jango is great when you have a wide range of items you would like to price. It provides a multitude of categories and narrowed-down subcategories.

- Jango uses more detailed search criteria than most price comparison search sites. After you select a category, you will be asked to supply manufacturer and model information. You are not required to provide this information, but the more specific your search criteria are, the more specific your search results will be.

- In addition to searching for pricing information, Jango also allows you to search for online reviews about a specific product. This feature is extremely helpful when considering a high-ticket purchase.

Other Price Comparison Search Sites

NetBuyer

http://www.zdnet.com/netbuyer/

- Netbuyer offers more searchable categories for price comparison than other sites, by far. Although it does not allow you to sort its search results list by price, it does contain the very useful Compare feature, which allows you to compare two or more vendors in a side-by-side format.

Shopping Network

http://www.lycos.com/emarket/shopping/

- Lycos, one of the top standard search sites, also contains a powerful price comparison Web page, which allows you to search by category and/or keyword. In addition, it contains a pull-down menu of options to help further narrow your keyword search.

Shopping Agents and Personal Shoppers

◆ Bid4it ◆ HotBot ◆ Other Sites

If you know exactly what you want but don't have time to go looking for it, use an Internet shopping agent. Simply submit a request to an Internet shopping agent, and the agent searches Web sites for the items that you request. Then the agent sends you a detailed description of the found items and their costs, and provides a direct link to Web stores where you can make your purchases.

Bid4it

http://bid4it.com

 Provide bid4it's Shopping Agent with your personalized information and it will do your shopping for you.

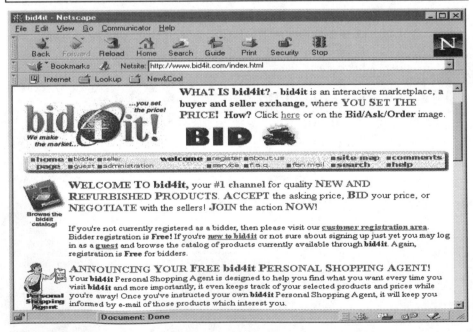

- The bid4it Web site allows you to specify a bidding price for a specific item, then matches your bid with current offers from various merchants.

- This sites' Personal Shopping Agent tracks products and prices for you even when you're not online. Bid4it requires that you become a member first. The membership form is quick and simple and allows you to be up and running (or bidding!) in a matter of minutes.

- When logging onto the bid4it Web site for the first time, you will be prompted for information. Click *Cancel*. This will allow you to view the site prior to becoming a member.

HotBot

http://shop.hotbot.com/

Tell the HotBot Shopping Agent how much you want to spend and it will match your request with a list of merchants.

- The HotBot shopping agent allows you to plug in information for the item you desire and then indicate the top price you are willing to pay. HotBot then displays manufacturers who are selling the item.
- Although the HotBot shopping agent is powered by the Junglee search engine, the advantage of this site over other sites is its ability to allow users to specify a maximum spending amount.

Other Sites

Helpmeshop.com

http://helpmeshop.com/

- This personal shopper is geared towards working folks who just don't have time to do random "real world" gift shopping.
- Many of the Web pages allow you enter a maximum dollar amount, in addition to other specifications.
- Check out the bakery-fresh online cheesecake—available for overnight shipping in a surplus of delicious flavors.

AMS Personal Shopper

http://ps.icw.com/Personal_Shopper/

- The AMS Personal Shopper is a feature of Access Market Square, the world's first cybermall. This free service will e-mail you reminders of important people and dates as well as provide special gift ideas from the online shops at Access Market Square.
- You may specify how many days in advance of the special occasion you wish to be notified, your gift price range, and a brief description of the person's favorite activities, foods, sports, and general likes and dislikes.

Make the Purpose

◆ Credit Cards ◆ Electronic Wallets
◆ CyberCash Wallet ◆ Microsoft Wallet
◆ Other Sites

Once you know what you want to buy, your next concern may be how to make the purchase. While some sites do accept personal checks or money orders, these payment methods will delay your order. For online purchases, your most efficient options are credit cards and electronic wallets.

Credit Cards

- Though it is not your only option, plastic definitely rules the Internet. It is the fastest and simplest way to making online purchases and most Web sites accept credit cards for purchases over $10.00.

- Credit cards provide the best protection against scams and fraudulent purchases. If a problem arises, you can always contest the charge, which is impossible to do if you pay by cash, check, or money order. In addition, there is a limit to your liability in any credit card related fraud. In most states, this limit is $50.

- Due to security concerns, some consumers still remain wary about giving credit card information over the Internet. When making a credit card purchase, look for the Better Business Bureau, NetWatch, or The Private Eye sign of approval. These services monitor Web sites for security and ethical business practices.

Electronic Wallets

■ An electronic wallet is a small downloadable software application that can be used to set up an online account for Internet purchases. It is filled with funds that you transfer from your own checking account, savings account, debit card, or credit card. These funds are then used to make safe, secure online purchases through a highly sophisticated encryption process, which makes it virtually impossible for anyone to obtain your personal information.

■ Though they use the same protection protocol, electronic wallets are operated by many different companies, including Microsoft and CyberCash, and they can be used for any or all of the following reasons:

- You do not have an active credit card.

- You are wary about using your credit card over the Internet.

- You want to make purchases for less than ten dollars. (Some Web sites only accept credit cards for purchases over $10.)

- You are using a Web site that does not recognize your Web browser.

CyberCash Wallet

http://www.cybercash.com/cybercash/wallet/

 CyberCash is the leader in digital commerce. The CyberCash Wallet can be used for large and small Internet purchases alike.

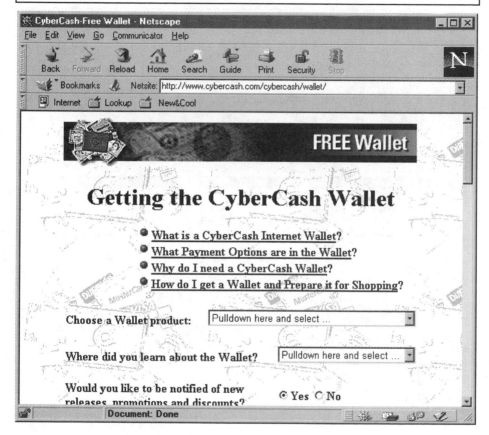

- CyberCash is the leading electronic wallet company. You can use your CyberCash Internet Wallet with CyberCash as well as CyberCoins. CyberCoin funds allow you to make purchases under $10.

- Once you download the CyberCash Wallet software, a simple set-up wizard will walk you through setting up a password and transferring funds from your checking, savings, credit, or debit accounts.

Microsoft Wallet

http://channels.microsoft.com/wallet/

 Make safe Internet purchase while simultaneously saving time and energy by using Microsoft Wallet.

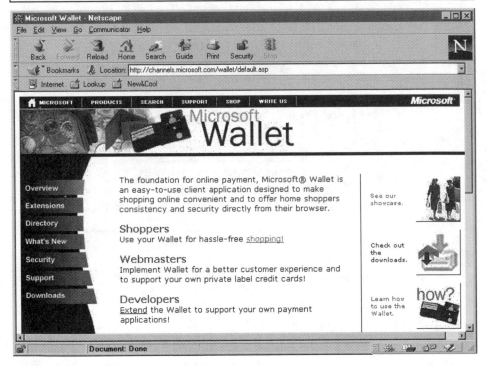

- This number one software company has added free, easy to download electronic wallet software to their surplus of computer applications. Several quality merchants and Internet malls participate in the service so you'll never run out of places to shop.

- The Microsoft Wallet provides an Address Control feature, which conveniently stores your ship-to and bill-to information. That means you won't waste time typing the same information over and over again at sites where you wish to make a purchase.

- If you're experiencing any problems with the Microsoft Wallet service, try checking out the link to the Microsoft Wallet Newsletter. The newsletter provides hints, tips, and additional information about Secure Electronic Transaction technology.

Other Sites

MilliCent Wallet

http://www.millicent.digital.com/discover/use/get /index.html

- MilliCent offers the same electronic wallet services as other companies do, however their specialty is smaller purchases, such as magazine articles, cartoons, music, video clips, online games, and software.

BlueMoney

http://www.bluemoney.com/comprod/products/ network_wallet.html

- BlueMoney works a little differently than other electronic wallets in that there is no software to download. You simply set up an ID and password at their Web site, and then you can use the BlueMoney Wallet whenever and wherever you want. This means you're not tied to making your purchases from a computer that contains electronic wallet software.

101 SHOPPING SITES

Apparel and Accessories

◆ **For the Whole Family** ◆ **Women** ◆ **Men**
◆ **Teens & Children** ◆ **Other Sites**

Electronic commerce is changing the way we do business—and that translates into huge savings for consumers. Because many merchants can sell to you at outlet or wholesale prices over the Net, you can save big bucks by shopping for clothes and accessories online. The middleman retailers—and their related costs—are cut out of the equation.

FOR THE WHOLE FAMILY

DESIGNEROUTLET.COM

http://www.designeroutlet.com/

 Find the finest quality items from nearly 100 of the world's best designers, at 35–75% savings.

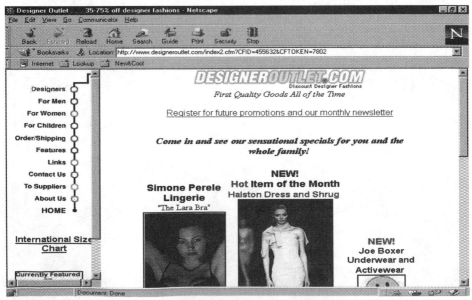

- You'll find great bargains for men, women, and children on overstocked items. New products arrive every two weeks—so you'll only find the most current season's merchandise.

- Take advantage of future promotions and additional discounts by registering at the site. Other great DESIGNEROUTLET.COM features include personal shoppers, gift boxes, special shipping requests, and 24-hour customer service.

One Hanes Place

http://www.onehanesplace.com

This online outlet specializes in name-brand hosiery, undergarments, active wear, plus sizes, and casual clothing for men, women, and children.

- Save 40%-50% off of retail prices every day with closeout sales and monthly specials. If you have questions or problems, e-mail customer service or call toll free.

- Check this site frequently to see what great buys are available in the Closeouts bin. These end-of-season items go like hot cakes, so you should act quickly if you find something you like.

The Sneaker Source

http://piano.symgrp.com/sneaker/index.html

 Run away with discounts of up to 50% (and more) on brand-name sneakers, including Adidas, New Balance, Nike, Puma, and more.

- For the best buys on top-selling sneakers, check out the Sneaker Source Sale Bin. Quantities are limited, but you can check frequently for new arrivals.
- Even the non-sale bin items cost less than the average retail price. The Sneaker Source has sporting goods and active wear, too.

- If you don't see what you're looking for, take advantage of customer service's JustRight™ policy. They handle special requests daily and strive to meet your needs.

Designers Direct®

http://www.designersdirect.com

 Looking for brand-name casual wear? Check out the current specials at this site for savings on big designer names like Calvin Klein, Levis, DKNY, and Tommy Hilfiger.

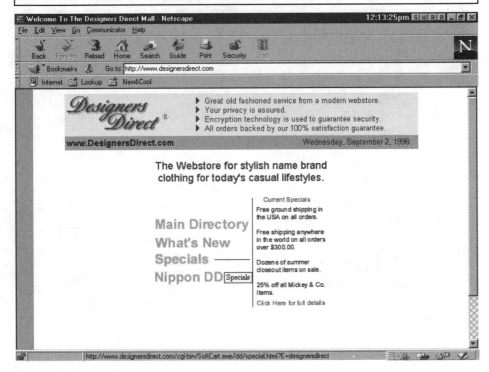

- Designers Direct sells overstock goods so you can buy the best clothes at incredibly affordable prices.

- All orders are backed with a 100% satisfaction guarantee, and toll-free, 24-hour, 7-day-a-week customer service will help you with gift purchases, special shipping requests, and exchanging goods for credit or merchandise.

WOMEN

Piece Unique^{SM}

http://www.pieceunique.com

If you are a "high-brow" bargain hunter, visit this site for a slice of otherwise unaffordable luxury.

- Do you have champagne taste on a soda budget? Now this must-see site lets you look like a model (or just dress like one). Get the best designer garments and accessories in mint condition at rock bottom prices.

- Piece Unique specializes in the resale of clothes that have been worn once or twice by actresses and models. This site updates inventory regularly with new arrivals.

Simply Southwest

http://www.simply-southwest.com/

For the finest in Southwestern apparel and accessories, Simply Southwest is an online outlet dedicated to bringing you factory-direct specials, overstocks, and warehouse closeouts.

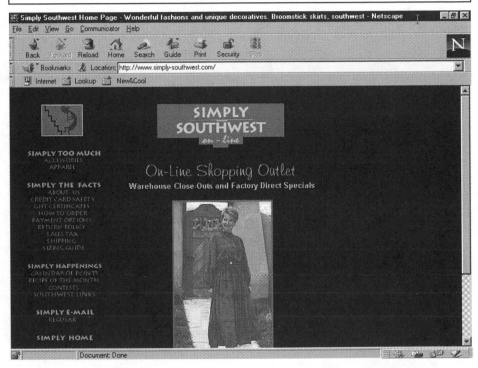

- Check the site frequently for weekly specials, bargains, contests, and other incentives on fine jewelry, handbags, scarves, and a large assortment of dresses, skirts, and casual wear.

- You can purchase your Albequerque apparel via secure server, call toll free, fax your order, or do it the old fashioned snail-mail way. You can get gift certificates for friends and savory southwestern recipes, too!

Rackes Direct

http://www.rackes.com/

Rackes Direct specializes in great deals on custom-made clothes for professional women.

- This award-winning site offers the discriminating shopper a personalized experience. Enjoy the experience of shopping at an exclusive boutique from the comfort of home. All items are competitively priced and often come with special coupons.

- All garments are made from knit and woven materials according to your preferences in color, style, and shape. Purchases include free home delivery.

MEN

Men's Collections Designer Outlet

http://mens.fcicom.com

Visit this site to save 50% or more on top name-brand casual wear for men.

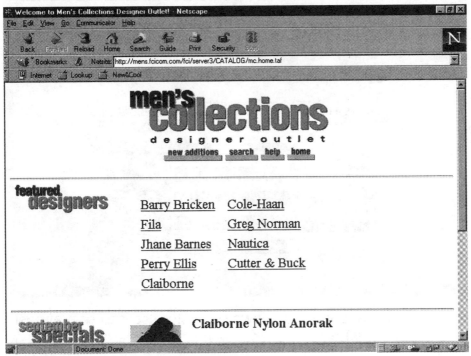

- In addition to regularly low-priced items from Perry Ellis, Cole-Haan, Claiborne, and Greg Norman, you'll find monthly specials at even lower prices.

- It pays to be the early bird at this site—especially to check out the monthly specials. These hot ticket items don't last long!

Hugestore.com

This award-winning site is home to the world's largest Internet shirt warehouse.

- "Self-service" shopping allows Hugestore.com to ship at cost, within $7 of wholesale prices, saving you 40%.

- Choose from a wide variety of shirts, ties, sport coats, and casual and dress pants. Select your fabric, fit, brand, and size (including big and tall), then fill out your order form. Your order is processed and packed in minutes.

Apparel Concepts for Men

http://www.apparelconcepts.com/

Get all your wardrobe basics—pants, coats, shirts, shoes, belts, socks, and underwear—at below retail prices at this just-for-men site.

A
P
P
A
R
E
L

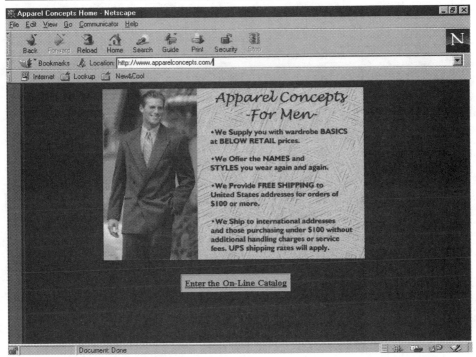

- If you can't find the style or size you're looking for, you can request a special order. You can place orders via fax, phone, or e-mail. If for some reason you're not satisfied with your purchase, this site honors a 30-day return policy.
- Order $100 or more and shipping is free.

TEENS & CHILDREN

moXiegirL

http://www.moxiegirl.com/

 For that special teenage girl with moxie, check out this ultimate cool site for excellent teen shopping.

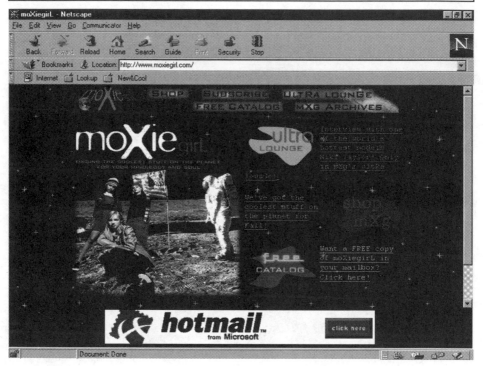

- This fun site for teenage girls is the online site related to the moXiegirL fashion catalog. Click the *Shop* link on the home page to order reasonably-priced teen fashions and accessories. Check the site frequently for discounts.

- This site also includes an Ultra Lounge for fashion tips, articles, and contributions from readers.

CWD: Children's Wear Digest

http://www.cwdkids.com/

This reputable catalog specializes in clothing for boys and girls sizes infant to 14.

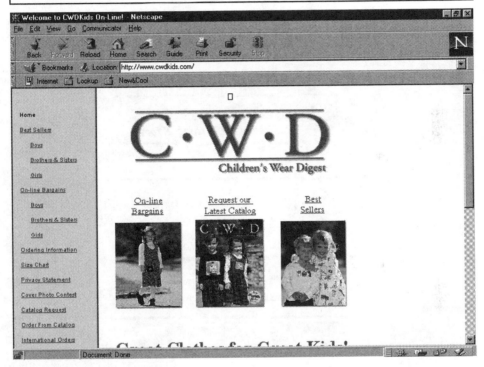

- From the home page, click *On-line Bargains* first to find special sales on name brands like Speedo, Flapdoodles, Cottontail Originals, and Sweet Potatoes.

- In addition to exclusive online bargains, you can enter your child in a cover photo contest, browse best-selling items, and request a CWD catalog. Call toll-free to order or use their secure online server.

WebClothes^{SM}.com

http://www.webclothes.com/

 This site features an extensive selection of children's clothing (sizes infant–7x) at 10%–50% below traditional retail prices.

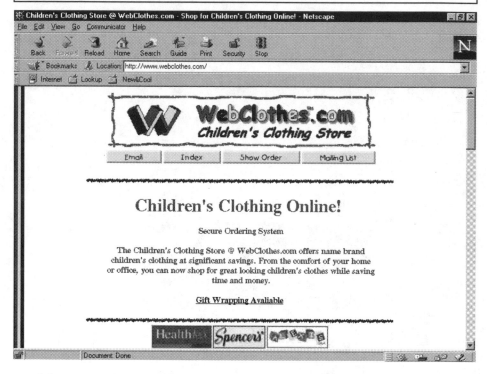

- After you view the low-priced specials featured on the home page, click the *Clothing Bargain Bin* link for close-out specials and other discounts. You'll find great prices, but act fast— items are limited and disappear on a first-come/first-serve basis.

- The Bargain Bin is updated daily, so check often. Gift wrapping and gift certificates are also available.

OTHER SITES

Clothesnet.Com

http://www.clothesnet.com

■ Do one-stop shopping for the whole family's wardrobe at this fantastic retail directory with hundreds of links to brand-name stores for men, women, teens, and children, you'll be sure to find what you're looking for here.

Fashionmall.com

http://www.fashionmall.com

■ If you want nothing but fashion, and want to shop from one secure, well-organized site, then visit Fashionmall.com, voted Best of the Web by Microsoft. You'll find designer items for women, men, teens, and kids. You can also shop for shoes, jewelry, beauty products, bridal accessories, media equipment, and more.

The Grocery Bag

◆ Food & Edibles ◆ Coffee, Tea, & Seasonings
◆ Wine & Beer ◆ Delectables ◆ Other Sites

Let the Internet bring you the most tantalizing flavors from all over the world in a matter of mouse clicks. Order live Maine lobster, *real* French bread (direct from Paris), and delicious Belgian chocolate truffles for dessert—and for less than restaurant prices! You'll also find tremendous savings online with your everyday groceries.

FOOD & EDIBLES

NetGrocer.com

http://www.netgrocer.com

 This premier (and very cool) virtual supermarket features nationwide delivery of thousands of low-priced groceries delivered directly to your home.

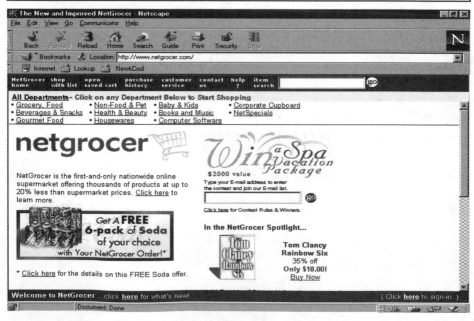

- Shop from a dozen departments, including gourmet, pet, health & beauty, housewares, kid's corner, and more. Just like at a real supermarket, you can view the products, read the labels, and get price per pound or ounce info. For quicker shopping, enter your shopping list and let NetGrocer round up your groceries for you.

- For even more savings, check out the NetGrocer's NetRewards Program for ways to stretch your grocery budget. Get points for shipping credits or frequent-flyer miles. If you want values galore for your everyday needs, put this site at the top of your bookmark list!

Crusoe Island Natural & Organic Grocery

http://www.crusoeisland.com

 Now you can visit your favorite health food store without even leaving home.

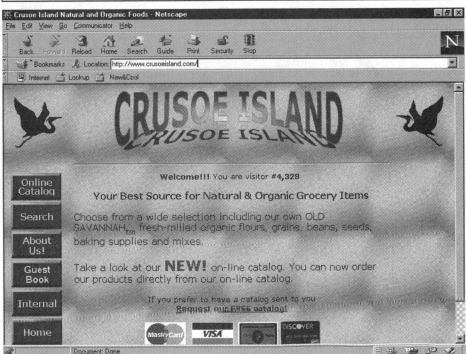

- This delightful site has a rich assortment of fresh-milled flours, grains beans, seeds, fruit juices, baking supplies, cookbooks, health and beauty products, vitamins, herbal remedies, and more.

- Although organic foods and products usually cost more, your best bet for savings is in the bulk foods department, where you can get goods at near wholesale prices. You can also get discounts on larger orders.

The Lobster Net

http://www.thelobsternet.com

 Even if you're nowhere near New England, you can have live (and feisty!) Maine lobsters shipped from the boat to your doorstep in 24 hours or less—at guaranteed lowest prices (shipping included).

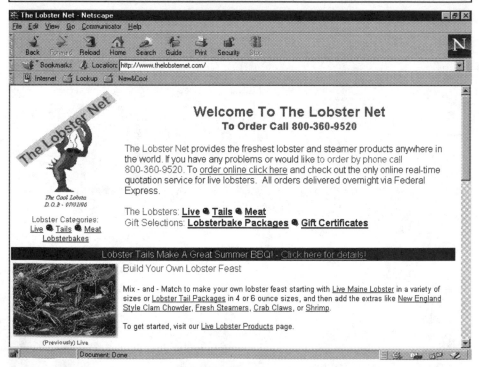

- If your mouth waters just at the thought of lobster tails and fresh steamers, then have some for dinner tomorrow night!

- You pick the quantity and size, and Lobster Net will quote you a price. Need help? Customer service is toll-free. Be sure to check out the featured specials, great recipes, and special gift baskets, too.

Farmer's Market Online

http://www.farmersmarketonline.com/

Visit this site for everything from specialty foods and produce to handmade items and books.

- In a word: WOW! If you're a fan of small farm goods and crafts, you'll love this "open air" market online. You buy directly from the vendor, so purchasing options vary.

- Enter monthly drawings to win $10 coupons good for any of the booth vendors. Also check the bulletin boards and forums for additional values, advice, and recipes. Or, go to the Auction Barn for everything from livestock to antiques to vehicles.

Peapod®

http://www.peapod.com

At Peapod, you can enjoy the luxury of personal shoppers without paying luxuriant prices.

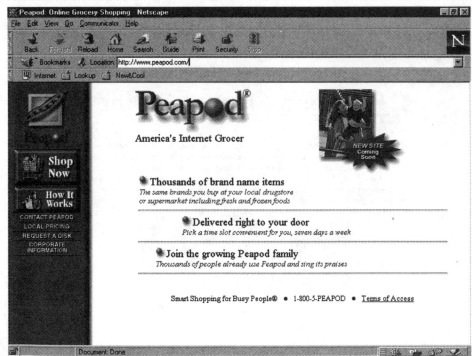

- You place your grocery order and Peapod shoppers do the legwork and deliver to your door. Use your own coupons, receive preferred customer savings, and always stay within your budget.

- If you find that the Peapod service is not yet available in your area, sit tight—they're currently in the process of going nationwide.

COFFEE, TEA, & SEASONINGS

Java Doc's Coffee Merchants

http://www.javadoc.com

For the ultimate cup of joe, you're bound to find the finest gourmet beans at Java Doc's at deliciously low prices.

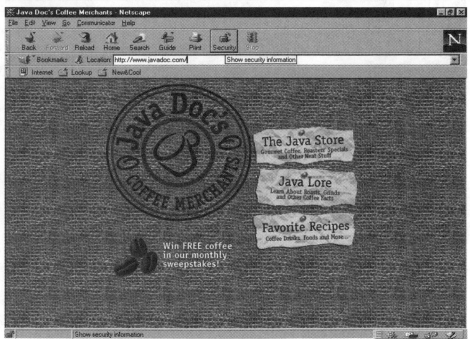

- Select your roast, then pick your grind: whole bean, coarse, medium, or fine.

- Click *JavaDoc's Specials* for your best bargain bets at this site. You'll also find flavored coffees, and coffee accessories. Order by phone, fax, or online.

The Best Coffee

http://www.thebestcoffee.com

 For superior blends from around the world, true connoisseurs will do well at this site.

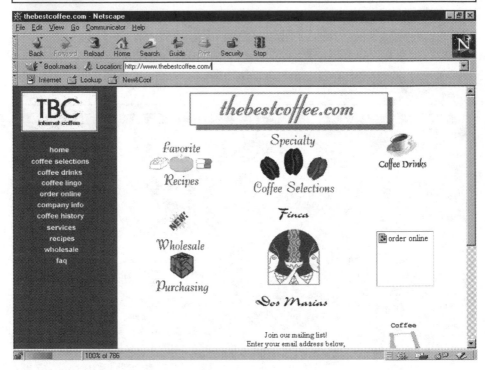

- Although The Best Coffee varieties are available for discount prices, you'll save the most money at this site by shopping wholesale (10 lbs. or more).

- 100% customer satisfaction is guaranteed at this secure site. You can also get up to speed on coffee lingo and drinks, and get fabulous recipes for cakes, tortes, cowboy beans, and other café goodies.

The Great American Spice Company, Inc.

http://www.americanspice.com

Shop for over 2,700 of the world's best loved exquisite spices, herbs, sauces, and seasonings at this savory site. Add some spice to your life with this site for food fans.

GROCERIES

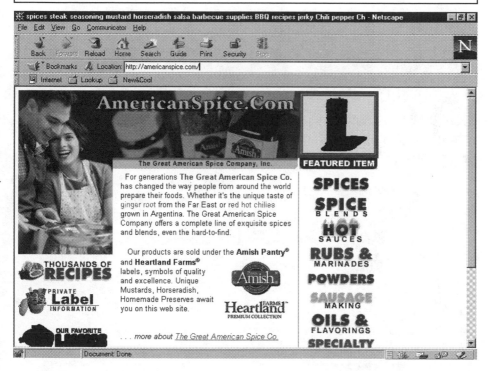

- Look for featured specials for great deals on yummy flavors. Discerning palates can even order custom blends.

- Get more than 20,000 free recipes and win prizes for submitting your own best creations. You can even get sausage making supplies and herbs and hard-to-find spices. All online orders are secure and safe.

Coffee Tea & Spice

**http://www.best.com/~blholmes/coffeeandtea/
coffeeandtea.shtml**

This San Francisco-based company has a wonderful variety of coffees and teas and gives a 10% discount on all orders. Plus, your order will be freshly roasted just for shipment.

- Whether you're tantalized by Tanzanian Peaberry or you swoon for Sumatra Mandheling, you'll find these and other roasts and blends at deliciously low prices. If tea is your bag, cozy up with a cup of chamomile or dozens of other varieties.
- Ordering is available via e-mail, toll-free phone, or fax. This site is also connected to some of San Francisco's best-loved shops in the Haight & Ashbury district.

WINE & BEER

Vickers' Liquors

http://www.vickersliquors.com

This family-owned and operated business out of Newport, Rhode Island features a huge selection of fine wines and hard-to-find vintages.

- Select from Wine Spectator's Top 100, or search by wine type, vintage, and price range.

- On-line shopping is still underway at this site, but in the meantime, you can contact the store by phone, fax, or e-mail.

Passport Wine Club

http://www.topwine.com/

If you like to enjoy the finest wines with your food, membership has its benefits at the Passport Wine Club.

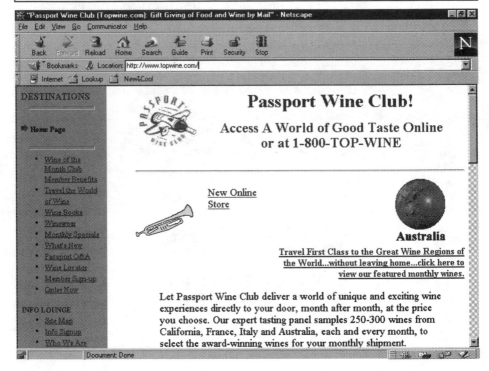

- Save up to 30% on the finest wines from all over the world and enjoy free shipping, handling, and packaging materials.
- Get great tips on wine varieties, check out monthly deals, and find great gifts for the other wine enthusiasts in your life.

Virtual Vineyards

http://www.virtualvin.com

 Find amazing wines for under $15 at this wine-lovers' online haven and enjoy browsing this visually appetizing award-winning site.

G
R
O
C
E
R
I
E
S

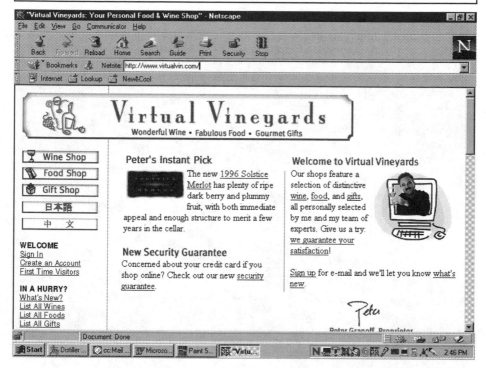

- Though wine is their specialty, you can also find fabulous foods, gifts, and other gourmet goodies here.

- Become a member, and you'll get instant notification of special buys, new features, and get VIP special services. Shopping is secure and satisfaction is guaranteed.

Sudsies

http://www.achilles.net/~awcook/

If you like to brew your own, check out this site for malts, wine kits, and brewing supplies at near wholesale prices.

- From the home page, click the *Specials* link to find out what's hot and what's on sale.

- This Canadian-based company guarantees the best exchange rates on all kits, spices, books, labels, and other home-brew necessities. Sudsies has a 30-day return policy on all goods and offers several methods for ordering. Get great tips and tricks, improve your beer and wine knowledge, and link to other resources.

DELECTABLES

Tropical's Nut House

http://www.tropicalnuthouse.com

If you're nuts about nuts, you can go wild at this site that features thousands of varieties of nuts, snacks, gourmet foods, candies, chocolates, and specialty foods.

- Get everything from adzuki beans to Zotz strings from a company that has been serving the country's finest chefs for over 20 years.

- Search for items by category or product name. Or, view the complete index and see all items listed with weight and price information. In addition to regular low prices, you can check out featured discounts, and register for monthly specials.

The Cookie Garden

http://www.cookiegarden.com/

Get sinfully delicious, ¼-pound (!) gourmet cookies made with the finest (and yummiest) all-natural ingredients that Cookie Monster would die for—all at a 10% savings at this site.

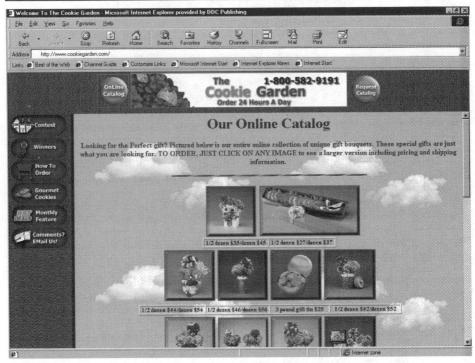

- If you're looking for a creative way to say "I love you," "Thank you," or "Congratulations," why not do it with an elegant box of long-stemmed…cookies! Browse through The Cookie Garden's mouth-watering selection of gourmet cookie gift baskets or simply order a tin for yourself.

- Serious cookie connoisseurs can enter a contest every two weeks for a chance to win a 3 lb. Gourmet Sampler. Check out the *Monthly Feature* link on the home page for additional hot deals. You can order these mouth-watering cookies for yourself or as a gift for a friend via online server, toll-free.phone, or fax.

The Fancy Foods Gourmet Club

http://www.ffgc.com

This award-winning site is a must-see for distinctive gourmands.

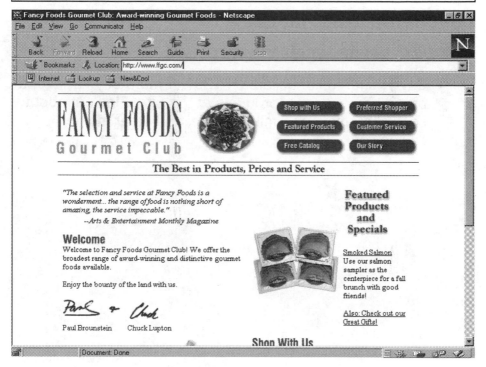

- At the Fancy Foods Gourmet Club, you can get the world's finest seafood specialties, pates, mousses, salsas, sweets, condiments, and other tasty treats at very competitive prices.

- Become a Preferred Shopper and get news of upcoming sales, featured products, and introductions to new gourmet items. You'll find impeccable customer service, and secure shopping options at this site.

OTHER SITES

Flying Noodle

http://www.flyingnoodle.com

- Pasta lovers of the world unite at this deliciously fun site. You'll love the artistic interface at Flying Noodle, and once you see all the gourmet pastas, sauces, olive oils, and other goodies, you'll love the site even more.

Coupon Clearninghouse

http://coupons.simplenet.com

- Save hundreds of dollars on 1200 or more of your favorite brand-name grocery products at this site. Find out about special promotions, limited offers, and other money saving tips.

Home & Garden

◆ Furniture ◆ Do-It-Yourself
◆ Kitchen, Bed, & Bath ◆ Garden Supplies

If you want to replace that rickety old rocking chair, renovate your bathroom with solid brass fixtures, or even dig a goldfish pond in your backyard, you'll find that improving your home and garden has never been easier. Now you can find high-quality shops that will help you transform your house into your castle without paying a king's ransom.

FURNITURE

affordablefurniture.com

http://www.affordablefurniture.com/

This site is the Mecca of online furniture shopping. Find brand-new, aftermarket, and close-out items at incredibly low prices.

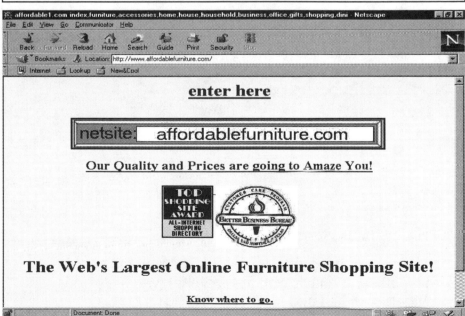

- The best place to start is the *Pricelist* link. You'll see a (very long) chart listing all items by category, product descriptions, and prices. Click on any link in the list to view the item.

- This site is very easy to navigate and gets two thumbs up on customer service. You can choose from five ordering options—all safe and secure. Satisfaction is guaranteed on all products. The best part: the already low prices include shipping and handling.

Alman's Home Furnishings

http://www.hickory.nc.us/ncnetworks/almans.html

 At Alman's Home Furnishings you save 40–50% off retail prices on major brands of furniture and home accessories.

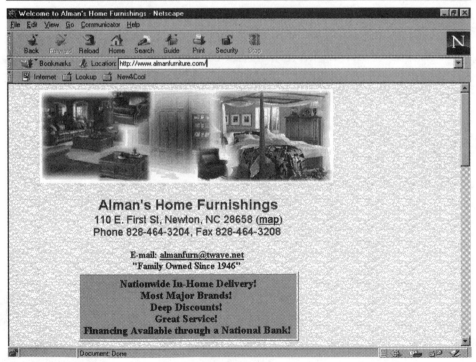

- Choose from hundreds of selections or submit special requests for furniture with the material (various woods, leather, or metal) and style of your choice.

- Orders may take anywhere from 10 days to three months, depending on availability. Alman's will repair or replace defective mechanical parts for life. Friendly customer service is available 8:30 a.m.–5:30 p.m. Eastern Standard Time.

Shaker Workshops®

http://www.shakerworkshops.com/

 This site offers the best prices on beautifully hand-crafted Shaker furniture, accessories, and specialty items. Save extra money by ordering furniture kits that you assemble at home.

H
O
M
E

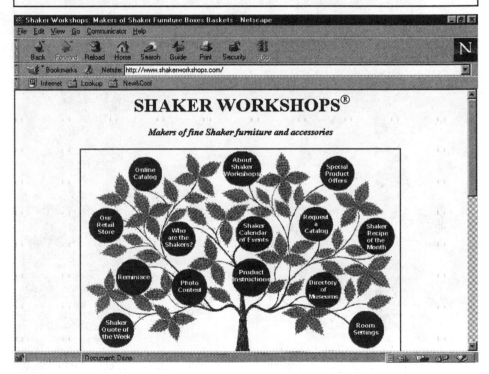

- Click the Online Catalog line to access directory of items. Then, click on an item to view the full details of each product available, including measurements and price.
- From the home page, click the *Special Product Offers* link to get additionally discounted furniture—either assembled or unassembled.

- Ordering is easy, either online or by phone, and goods are delivered within 10 business days of your order. Shaker Workshops honors a 30-day return policy.

Woodtown Unfinished Furniture

http://www.woodtownusa.com/

 Woodtown sells unfinished Mission-style bedroom sets, garden and patio furniture, tables, armoirs, chairs, and more at incredibly low prices.

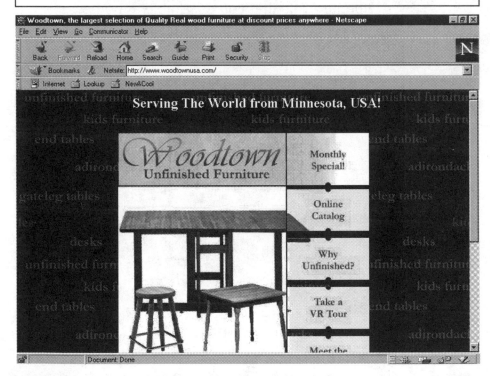

- This Mom and Pop furniture store out of Elk River, Minnesota has been making and selling fine quality, very reasonably priced, unfinished furniture for more than 20 years. Choose from. When you buy unfinished wood, you get higher quality wood (nothing to cover up the nicks and dings), and you can mix and match furniture and choose your own colors.

- Online ordering is not currently available, but you can print out an order form, fill it out, and fax it directly to Woodtown. You can also call in orders.

DO-IT-YOURSELF

CyberFaucet

http://www.cyberfaucet.com/

 This may be the best place on the Web to find the highest quality faucets, fixtures, sinks, and accessories at the lowest prices.

H
O
M
E

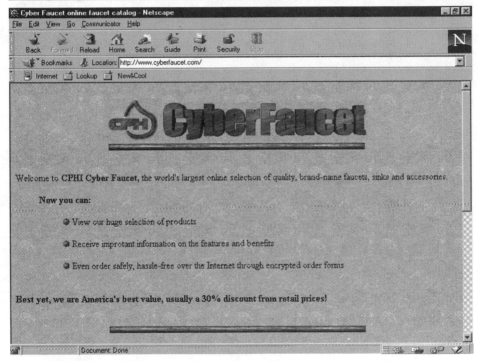

- At CyberFaucet, you'll save at least 30% from retail prices on all items, and even more on clearance items. CyberFaucet offers the finest materials, including solid brass, ceramic, chrome, gold, and custom finishes. If you have specific requests, make a custom order and CyberFaucet will hunt down the lowest prices nationwide for you.

- Once you get your goods, you can always contact technical support for questions you may have about installation issues or product conflicts.

CyberBath™

http://www.baths.com/

All your bathroom needs can be met at this discount online plumbing site.

- Whether you want a clawfoot bathtub or a new soap dish, CyberBath offers luxury kitchen and bath fixtures at guaranteed unbeatable prices. And you don't have to pay delivery fees within the continental U.S.

- Check out the closeouts and overstock items for additional savings. You can "thumb through" the site like a catalog, to view all featured products, or use the search feature to find specific items. Order via secure server, phone, fax, or e-mail.

Coastal Tool & Supply

http://www.coastaltool.com/

"The Discount Tool People" have the widest selection of brand-name hand and power tools available on the Web.

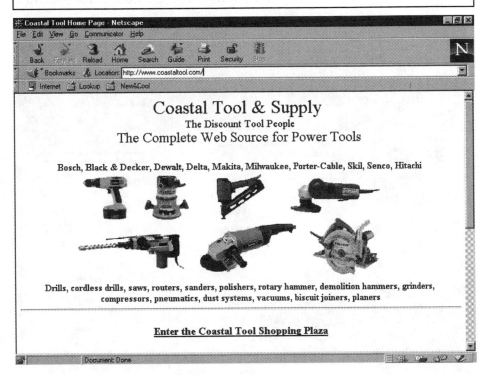

- This handsome site is straightforward and easy to navigate. Find what you're looking for fast, and if you can't, customer service will find it for you.

- In addition to all your favorite tools at the lowest possible discount prices, you'll find great gift ideas and specials, freebies, and special features. Make safe and secure purchases with 100% satisfaction guaranteed.

KITCHEN, BED, & BATH

bedandbath.com

http://www.bedandbath.com/

 This home accessories site carries brand-name products at all the low prices.

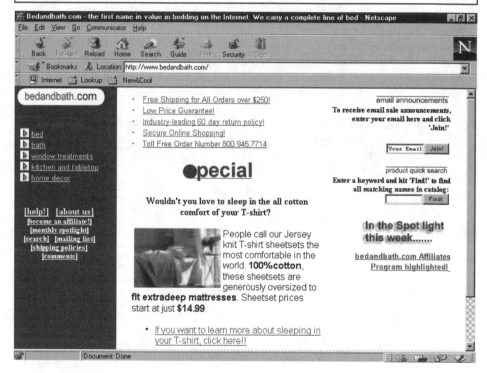

- Shop from a huge assortment of fashion bedding ensembles, sheets, pillows, comforters, bath towels and accessories, window treatments, kitchen linens, and home décor at this discount site.

- Bedandbath.com guarantees the lowest prices on all your purchases. If you find a better deal, bedandbath.com gives you the difference plus 5%. If you make a purchase of $250 or more, you won't have to pay for shipping. Bedandbath.com honors a 60-day return policy.

Blind Ambition Window Coverings

http://www.blindambition.com/

Save hundreds of dollars by paying wholesale prices on name-brand mini-blinds, wood blinds, shades, and more at Blind Ambition Window Coverings.

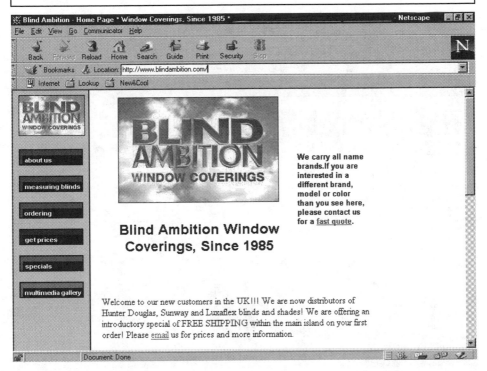

- With more than a million items in stock, you're sure to find the right window coverings for every window in your home at this site. You can select your colors, measurements, brand, model, and price in one online session from any page at this site. If you need to see actual colors (versus what you see on your computer screen) Blind Ambition Window Coverings will send you up to three swatch cuttings at no charge.

- Be sure to check out the *Specials* link for additional savings, rebates, bargains, and limited offers. You may order via check, credit card, or money order.

The Internet Kitchen

http://www.your-kitchen.com/

 At the Internet Kitchen site, you can fill your kitchen without emptying your wallet.

- This award-winning and certified safe shopping site features dozens of brand-name kitchen products at discount prices. Shop for cookbooks, cookware, cutlery, gadgets, fabrics, canning materials, and more.

- New products and special deals are featured on the home page. You can also click the *Special Offers* link to take advantage of monthly specials and giveaways, brand-name discounts, and free trial issues of magazines. Free shipping is available for all orders of $300 or more.

No Brainer Blinds and Shades

http://www.nobrainerblinds.com/

If you want custom crafted, name-brand blinds or shades, you're guaranteed to get them here at rock-bottom prices.

H O M E

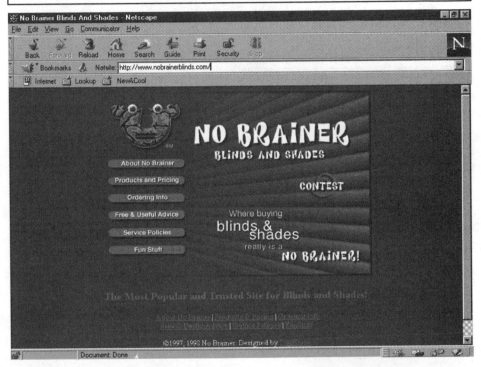

- No Brainer Blinds and Shades carries a huge inventory and promises to beat any competitors price. Be sure to check out the Web Special link which offers regularly updated bargain basement specials.

- You can also get detailed measuring tips, installation advice, and movie tutorials—not to mention their toll-free customer service. Orders are shipped directly from the factory within one day of your order. Pay no shipping and no sales tax outside of Texas. All products come with a lifetime warranty.

- This hip site comes with a sense of humor and numerous accolades. Check out the Fun Stuff link for a few online chuckles before you leave.

Cuddledown of Main

http://www.cuddledown.com/

 From comforters, to towels, to bedroom furniture this site has it all.

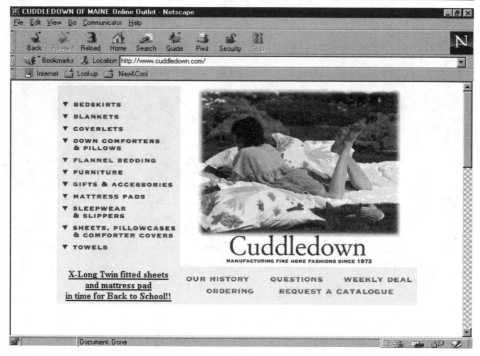

- This 25-year old company now features special discounts to online customers. Search this site for overstocked high quality bedding, blankets, linens, pillows, towels, sleepwear, comforters, and other accessories at marked down prices.

- Click the *Weekly Deal* link on the home page for limited featured specials. Click the *Questions* link for detailed information about down and other materials used in their products.

- You can order these special discounted products either via toll-free fax or e-mail. All merchandise is guaranteed 100%— for refunds or credit if you're dissatisfied.

GARDEN SUPPLIES

Burpee Seed Company

http://garden.burpee.com/

 From seeds to garden tools to lawn furnishings, this site can meet all garden and lawn needs.

G
A
R
D
E
N

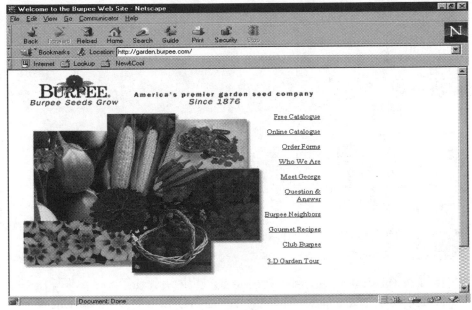

- Now you can get the most out of one of the oldest and most trusted names in gardening since 1876. If you're a serious gardener, you can really take advantage of this site by joining Club Burpee. You'll get special online discounts and sales, free products, and new catalog releases.

- From the home page, click *Online Catalog* to shop. View featured products and specials, browse categories, and enjoy safe and secure ordering. In addition to all the great garden seeds and supplies, you can get gourmet recipes and free horticultural advice.

Discount Pumps & Liners

http://www.pacificcoast.net/~ponds/index.htm

 Now it's easy and inexpensive to create your own garden pond by shopping at the Discount Pumps and Liners site.

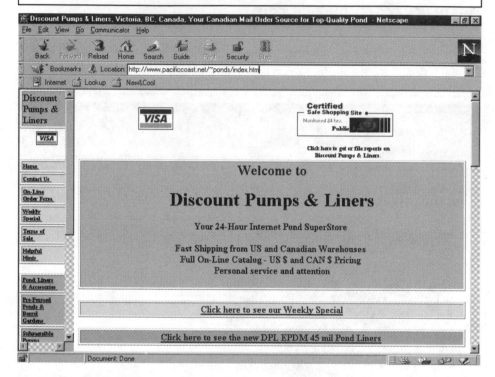

- If your ultimate garden includes a goldfish pond with lily pads or a statuesque water fountain, then come to this cyber-superstore for up to 40% off all your water garden needs.

- Get the best pond liners, pumps, fountain heads, underwater lighting, plant baskets, fish foods, filters, and more. Before browsing the huge selection, check out the weekly specials, where you can get even better deals on already discounted items.

garden.com

http://www.garden.com/

An ultimate site for all green thumbs, here you can find everything from gardening products to personalized garden design.

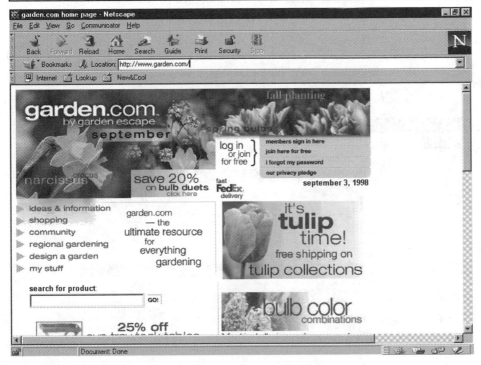

- Find tremendous specials featured on the home page, chat with expert gardeners, learn what's best for your garden, and browse articles.

- To take full advantage of this online service, become a member for free and get 20% off of your first purchase, receive their on-line magazine, get customized help for your region, and get all the VIP services.

LandscapeUSA

http://www.landscapeusa.com

This is the ultimate one-stop shopping site for gardening tools and supplies, landscaping and irrigation needs, outdoor furniture, books, clothing, and other backyard bonanzas.

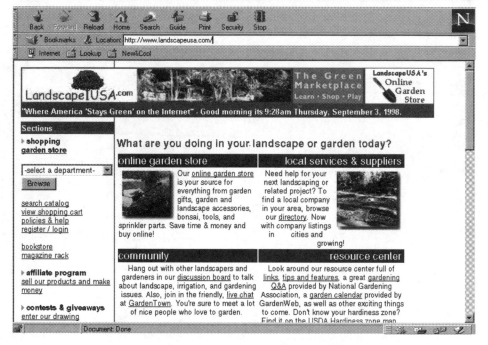

- Sales, discounts, and specials are featured on the home page, as are links to every shopping department. You can view images and read complete descriptions of all products. Shipping is free on all orders of $100 or more.

- In addition to providing the largest selections of lawn and garden products online, LandscapeUSA also has a discussion board where you can post messages, get advice, and read about what others are planting in their backyards.

Flowers & Gifts

◆ Flowers ◆ Gifts ◆ Cigars ◆ Collectibles
◆ Other Sites

Whether your Aunt Judith in Juneau is having a birthday (tomorrow!) or your eccentric Uncle Oliver can't smoke enough cigars, getting unique gifts for family and friends has never been easier. Now you can find more amazing gifts than you can dream up at completely affordable prices right at your fingertips.

FLOWERS

1st in Flowers

http://www.1stinflowers.com

This site is more than just flowers; check out the reasonably priced gourmet items and gifts.

- This exquisite site has rotating specials, plants, flowers, gourmet items, and gifts for every occasion. Stretch your flower power by clicking the Best Values link to see featured specials.

- Same day delivery is available if you place your order before noon within the same time zone to which you wish to send your gift. If you need a little extra help remembering an occasion, take advantage of the free reminder service. This award-winning site is safe and secure.

2G Roses: Access the Grower

http://www.freshroses.com

 For bountiful bouquets at unbelievably low prices buy your flowers straight from the source— the growers.

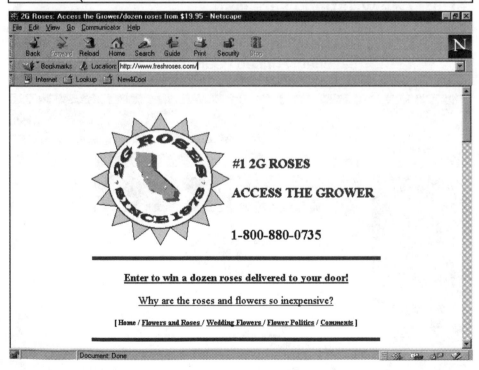

- At the 2G Roses site, you purchase your flowers directly from the growers. Because they ship the flowers to you direct, there is no middle man to pay. You'll be hard pressed to find cheaper or fresher flowers unless you grow them yourself. This site specializes in volume purchases for weddings and festive events, but their everyday long stem roses and table flowers are not to be surpassed. Have 2G Roses help you take advantage of what's in season to get the most bloom for your buck.

The Village Gardens

http://www.villagegardens.com

 The Village Gardens site offers an easy way to purchase quality flowers, plants, and specialty arrangements with a few mouse clicks.

- Whatever the occasion, you're sure to find some of the best prices on roses, arrangements, and plants, 24 hours a day, 7 days a week. Click on a picture of an arrangement or plant to view the item, plus get complete descriptions and pricing information.
- You can also get great flower care tips and free reminder services. Same day delivery is also available. You can order via secure server, toll-free phone, or fax.

GIFTS

AAAA Gifts

http://www.aaaagifts.com

This gift-themed megasite is sure to carry something for everyone on your gift list.

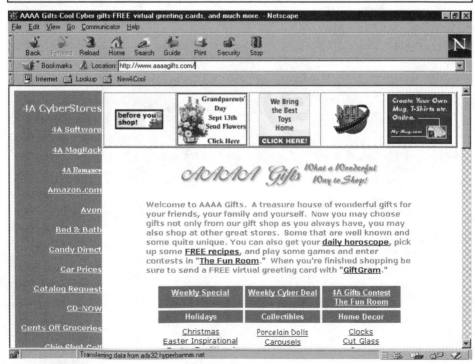

- For a complete treasure-trove of truly unique gifts at up to 50% off of catalog prices, you can find something for everyone at this mammoth shopping site.

- Bargain hunters should start by checking the *Weekly Specials*, *Weekly Cyber Deals*, *Bag a bargain*, and *Supermarket specials* links on the home page. Also be sure to check out the free recipes, weekly auctions, monthly contests, and free gifts with every order.

C.I.M. Group

http://www.cimgroupgems-jewelry.com

At the C.I.M. Group Web site, you can shop for fine jewelry, antiques, and other gifts right from the comfort of your home—and save money doing it.

- This secure site offers gemstones and jewelry from all over the world at prices below retail market. Click the *Specials* link from the home page to get great deals on gems and jewels, participate in monthly bids, and enter a monthly drawing for free gems.

- Find out detailed information about gems, including origins, meanings, birthstones, and more. This certified safe shopping site also has a fine selection of antiques, collectibles, and one-of-a-kind items.

The Baby Catalog of America

http://www.babycatalog.com

 For brand-name baby and toddler gifts, its hard to beat The Baby Catalog of America's Web site, which boasts a phenomenal inventory of rock bottom prices.

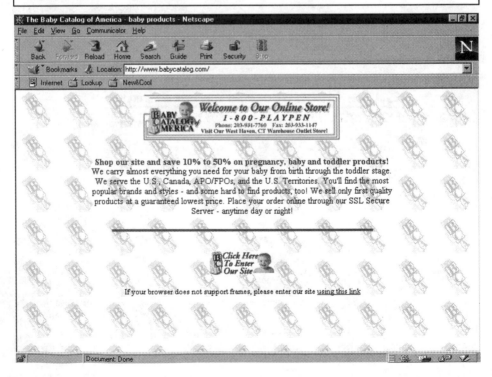

- Looking for newborn gifts that don't cost grown-up prices? This site has 10–50% off of baby gifts, toddler needs, and pregnancy products. If you're not sure what to get the mother-to-be, get a gift certificate. Click the *Specials* link for super-low prices and free shipping offers.

- No matter what the item, this site guarantees the lowest prices. So if you find a better price, they'll match it. If you know you're going to be doing a lot of baby shopping, take advantage of The Baby Club Savings Program, where you get an addition 10% off of all purchases.

CIGARS

TheSmokeShop.Com

http://www.thesmokeshop.com/

 A cigar lover's dream, this site has an impressive collection of cigars by the box, bundle, or stick.

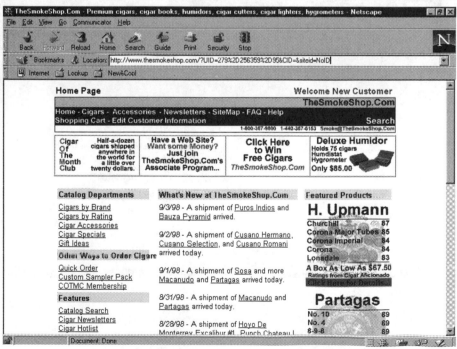

G
I
F
T
S

- At this specialty site, which mainly focuses on cigars, you'll find a comprehensive selection of cutters, lighters, humidors, and other essential accessories.

- In addition to regular specials, Cigar Of The Month Club members get even better deals. Look on the home page for new shipments listed by date of arrival. Also find great features including newsletters, hotlists, contests, custom packs, and ratings from *Cigar Aficionado*.

Corona Cigar Company

http://www.coronacigar.com

Find what you're looking for quickly and easily at this easy-to-navigate site that specializes in cigar sales.

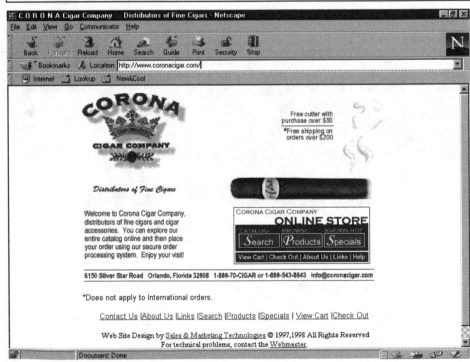

- To search for your dream cigar, use the powerful Catalog Search engine, which allows you to search by maker, country of origin, product description, and keyword(s). Click the *Products* link for a complete index of all items listed by brand and price. Find smokin' hot specials and discount prices, too.

- Cigar of the Month Club members get an additional 10% off of all purchases. This site promises only the finest hand-made cigars, and backs that with a complete money-back guarantee. Free shipping is available for orders totaling $200 or more.

The Tobacco Shop of Ridgewood

http://www.tobaccoshop.com/

This New Jersey shop has a large inventory of the world's finest cigars, including Avo, Padron, Savinelli, and Cohiba. You'll also find over 40 blends of pipe tobaccos and accessories.

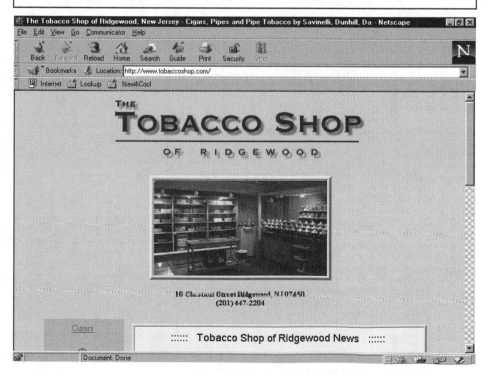

G I F T S

- Looking for a rare cigar or unique accessory? Submit your request and they'll find it for you. Click the *Catalog Index* for a complete inventory, including closeout specials of up to 50% and more off regular prices.

- If you live outside of New Jersey, there are no tobacco taxes to pay, which can mean steep savings.

COLLECTIBLES

The Internet Antique Shop Mall

http://www.tias.com/

This award-winning site features new dealers, inventory, specialty sites, and live online auctions for specific items daily.

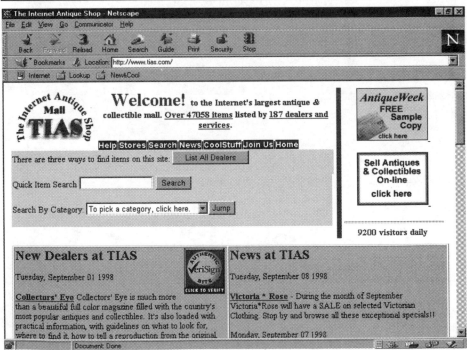

- With over 63,000 antiques and collectibles listed by hundreds of dealers and services, The Internet Antique Shop Mall is by far the largest such mall on the Web.

- You'll also find hundreds upon hundreds of books and periodicals devoted solely to antiques and collectibles. Although all listed vendors are TIAS members, you conduct all auctions, purchases, and other transactions at each Web site you link to from TIAS. Purchasing options vary from site to site.

Wood's Antiques & Collectibles

http://www.zianet.com/woods/

When the standard gift just won't do, try Wood's Collectibles for something rare and different.

G
I
F
T
S

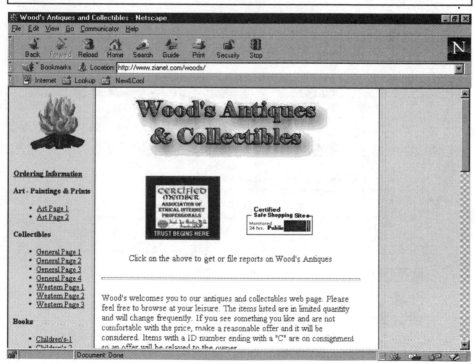

- Find books, art, toys, radios, Disneyana, china, glass, Beanies, and more at this extensive site. If you see something you like at a price you don't, make Wood's an offer and you might get lucky .

- Inventory turns around quickly here, because quantities are limited. You can request to be notified when new, specific items come in stock. For real steals, see what items are in the Garage Sale pages, where everything is priced at $5.00.

Funk & Junk[SM]

http://www.funkandjunk.com/

 Let Funky J. Monky[SM] be your guide through the thousands of antiques and collectibles at this wacky site.

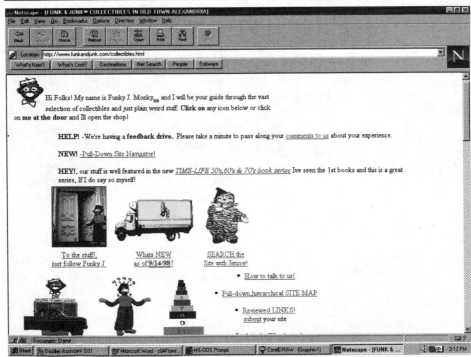

- At the Funk & Junk web site you'll find featured sale items, top ten best picks, and a warehouse full of vintage clothing, dolls, toys, pottery, records, lamps, jewelry, and books, just to name a few.

- Check for new arrivals, search for something in particular, or "Ask Elle" any questions you may have about collectibles. You'll find competitive prices at Funk & Junk, whose motto is "Cool Stuff for Cool People at Cool Prices[SM]." Ordering is available by phone, fax, mail, or e-mail.

OTHER SITES

Hillary's Personalized & Handpainted Gifts
http://www.hillarysgifts.com

- This site has received numerous awards and accolades, and for a good reason, too. If you want to send something personal, Hillary's will help you create a unique present within your budgetary demands. You'll find a wide variety of custom gift baskets and goodies for him, her, kids, couples, home, and work. Express shipping and gift-wrapping is also available at this secure shopping site.

Spree.com
http://www.spree.com/

- This massive superstore has a notable collection of gift baskets, games, toys, flowers, movies, music, books, and electronic items. If you're looking for gifts in general, this is a great site to browse. Every single item is marked down to a discount price.

Wholesale Shopping
http://www.wholesaleshopping.com

- This discount marketplace has tons of housewares, electronics, gifts, and other items for up to 70% off of retail prices. Save an additional 10% on all items when you become a Discount Club Member.

Entertainment

◆ Music ◆ Movies and Video ◆ Books ◆ Art

No need to spend hours seeking means of entertainment. With countless music, movie and video, and art-related sites available on the Internet, you can let entertainment come to you! Many entertainment sites provide online audio and video samples, so don't miss out on the fun.

MUSIC

CD Gigastore

http://www.gigastore.com/cgi-bin/record/

 By far one of the largest music inventories on the Web, this site boasts over 160,000 discounted CD and video titles.

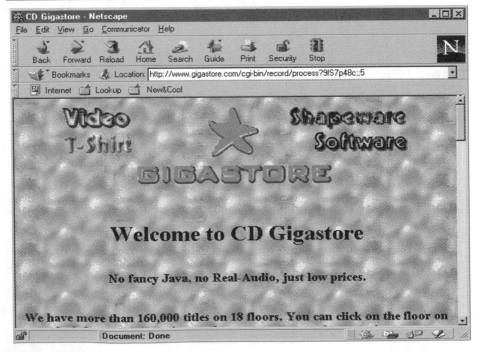

- All you need is a CD title or an artist's name to start your search. CD Gigastore will list music products (CDs, cassettes, and LPs) within moments. You can choose to sort the list by price, title, or artist.

- You can browse through just about every imaginable genre of music at CD Gigasite. Links to everything from holiday music to jazz to heavy metal are available from the home page, so you won't waste time sifting through music that may not appeal to you.

CD World

http://www.cdworld.com/

 If you're looking for variety as well as discounts, the selections at this site will make you sing.

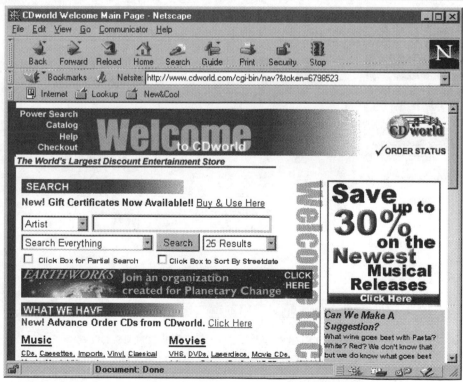

- Although CD World specializes in music, this entertainment power-site also carries a large inventory of discount movies, video games, and software.

- To search through all mediums, select artist, title, song, or soundtrack from the pull-down menu, type a desired keyword (such as a singer's name) and wait for your search results.

CDnow

http://www.cdnow.com

Definitely one of the most popular music sites on the Web, CDnow features variety as well as volume.

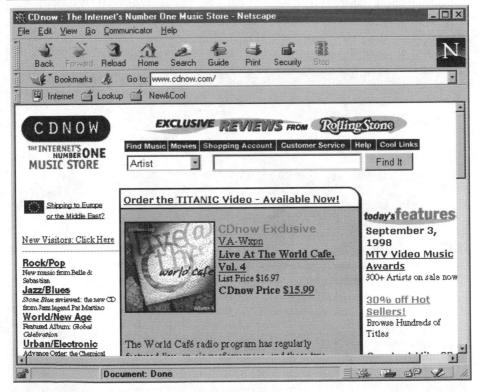

- CDnow regularly offers 30% off of retail prices on most items. In addition, this site provides live audio samples and reviews of several hot new music releases.

- Check out the regularly updated music news and discount specials that are announced daily on Cdnow's home page. A definite favorite is the *Greatest Hits* selections for $9.99 or less.

MOVIES AND VIDEO

Discount Video

http://www.gigastore.com/cgi-bin/record/

 This site specializes in older movies and television, as well as foreign movies.

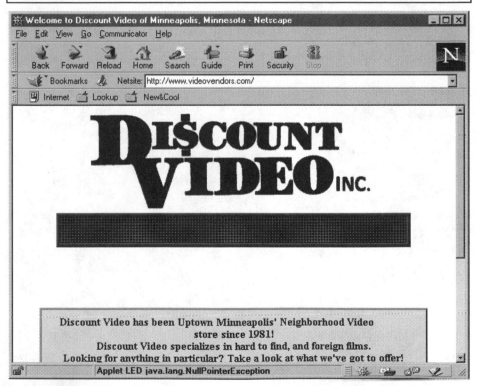

- Looking to buy a copy of a movie or TV show that aired ten or so years ago? Look no further! Discount Video not only offers unbelievable prices, but their inventory is amazing!

- And in case you're a trivia buff, links to all actors and cast members are also available at each TV or movie Web site. You can find out other movies and TV shows featuring a favorite actor, director, or make-up artist simply by clicking their name.

Videoserve.com

http://www.videoserve.com/

This site boasts over 140,000 titles at remarkable prices.

- At this bargain movie site, most selections are sold at rock-bottom prices, close to 40% off what you might pay at a retail location in the "real world."

- The Expert Search feature allows you to search for films by performer, director, producer, or genre.

- Be sure to check out the *Cost Cutter Movies* link, which offers fifty movies that are currently selling for less than ten dollars. But don't stop here. Countless other movies are also offered at unbelievable prices.

Laser Movies

http://www.gigastore.com/cgi-bin/record/

Laser Movies sells movies for laser disc and DVD technology at all-time low prices.

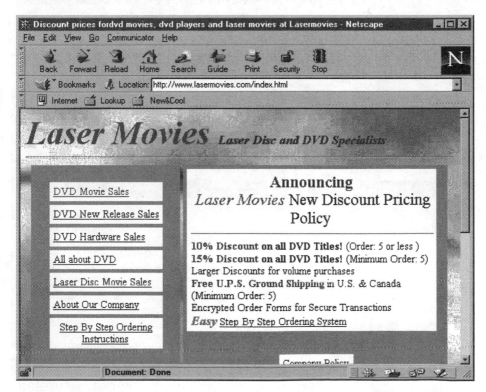

- Though their inventory is not huge, Laser Movies prices are better than many video shops (online or off). They regularly offer 10%–15% off on all titles and their free shipping policy makes this site a double bargain.

- Laser Movies is fast and simple. You won't get tangled up in gimmicks or various links to other Web pages when you use this sight to purchase your movies.

BOOKS

Amazon.com

http://www.amazon.com

As the ruler of online booksellers, Amazon.com beats just about every other store's book prices.

- The title of this Web site speaks for itself. This company is giant: giant selection, giant discounts, and giant visibility. Even when you think you're buying a book from a smaller online company, the company may actually be operated by Amazon.com. (Look for the trademark symbol!)

- It's hard to beat the Amazon.com home page, which features a powerful search engine (for locating almost any book imaginable and at unimaginable discounts of up to 60%), music selections, suggested reading, and so much more.

Hamiltonbook.com

http://www.hamiltonbook.com

 A no-frills bookstore site offering discounts that match those normally only offered at the bigwig book sites.

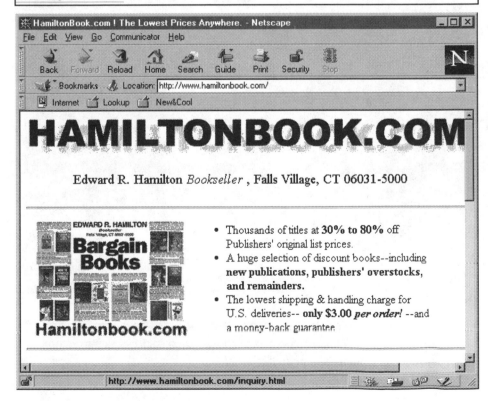

HAMILTONBOOK.COM

Edward R. Hamilton *Bookseller* , Falls Village, CT 06031-5000

- Thousands of titles at **30% to 80%** off Publishers' original list prices.
- A huge selection of discount books--including **new publications, publishers' overstocks, and remainders.**
- The lowest shipping & handling charge for U.S. deliveries-- only $3.00 *per order!* --and a money-back guarantee

http://www.hamiltonbook.com/inquiry.html

- The simplicity of this Web site is one of its best qualities. Though the selection is tremendous and the discounts are large, this site contains the charm of a local bookstore.

- Green ticket items reflect normally discounted books (usually up to 30%) and red ticket items reflect even deeper discounts due to publisher's closeouts and overstocking.

Riverrun Books

http://www.riverrun-books.com

 More than just your average bookstore, Riverrun Books is an all-in-one bargain bookstore and literary hangout.

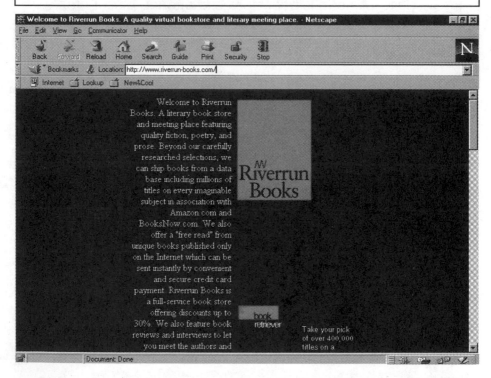

- Unlike most online bookstores, this site offers some special touches, such as author interviews, detailed book reviews, and online fiction and poetry.

- The literary bent of this beautifully designed Web site continues with the Weekly Features, which are chosen for content, and not for quantity of units sold. But don't be mistaken: you can get a mean discount on all books—and it's easy as pie to place your order.

ART

Art 4 Less

http://www.art-4-less.com

At Art 4 Less, liquidation is king. Purchase unique art from the comfort of your computer without going bankrupt.

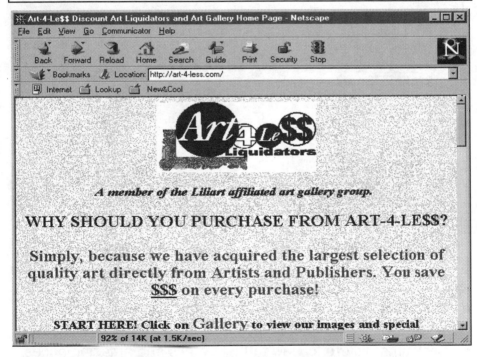

- This site does exactly what its title indicates: sells art for bargain prices. You can view pictures of each piece, and read about the artist's history, the medium used to create the piece, and its price (retail versus discount).

- Don't forget to check out the *Special Offers* link, which links you to rock-bottom art deals as well as some free giveaways.

Roman Art

http://www.romanart.com

This unique Web site is dedicated to selling beautiful Roman art sculptures at reasonable prices.

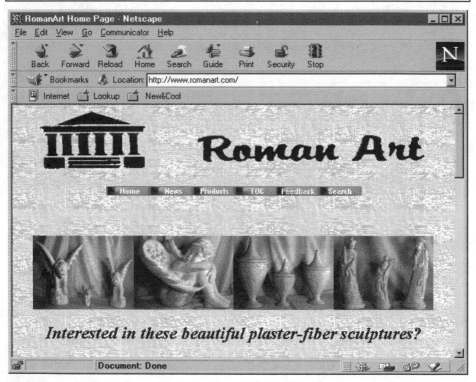

- The plaster-fiber sculptures sold at this site are available for both interior and exterior display.
- Click on a picture to view further details and amazing prices. Ordering these beautiful sculptures is quick and painless with the company's online order form.

The Art Market

http://www.artmarketplace.com/

The Art Market guaranties unbeatable art at unbeatable prices—or your money back.

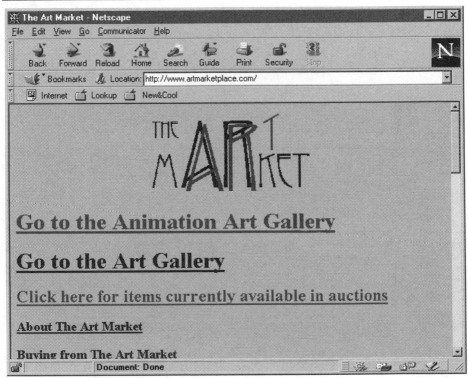

- The Art Market is number one when it comes to selling animation art online. Their inventory is warehouse-sized and brimming with rare deals on original production cels, pencil drawings, and more.

- Check out the Art Gallery section for classic, rare pieces by famous artists. It's hard to imagine that you can actually buy a 17th-century painting over the Internet, but you can at The Art Market Web site—and receive a wonderful discount while doing so.

Electronics

◆ Audio and Video
◆ TVs and Cameras ◆ Computers

There are countless electronics stores on the Web these days.
Sure you can buy a stereo, television, VCR, camcorder, or
computer from any of these sites—but when you're making a
high-ticket purchase, you want to find a quality site, with quality
guarantees, and the lowest-of-low prices.

AUDIO AND VIDEO

AmDEX

http://www.go-amdex.com/

This popular megasite offers one-stop shopping
for all audio and video needs, in addition to other
electronic products.

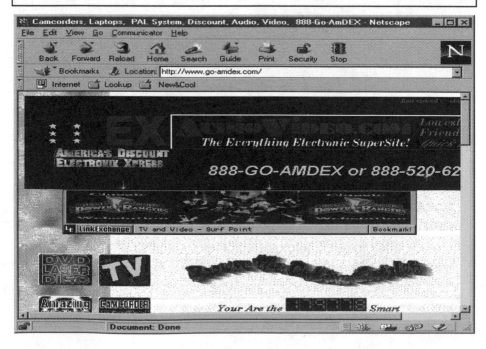

- AmDEX provides detailed descriptions and pictures of all their audio and video products. Simply click on a picture link to access a desired category. Then choose a brand and an array of products and pictures display.

- Be sure to scroll to the bottom of each category page to view current bonus discounts.

Ben's House of Electronics

http://www.emrkt.com/estore/ben/

This specialized site focuses on audio and stereo equipment but also sells various electronic goods.

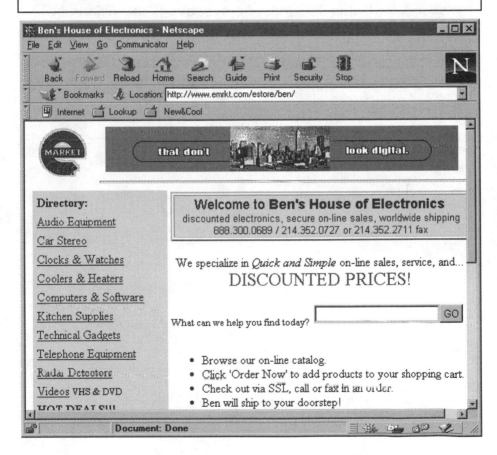

- Ben's House of Electronics is super easy to use. Just type a product description into the search box and press Go! A list of matching products is displayed along with 1 to 4 gold stars. The number of stars presented indicates how closely the result may match your request.

- Don't forget to click on the *HOT DEALS* link from the home page to view a list of discounted electronics from all categories.

TVS AND CAMERAS

Sutter Telecom

http://www.suttertel.com/electronics.html

Sutter Telecom offers a bevy of television and video equipment at unbelievable prices.

- This site may not offer the wide variety of some other electronics sites, but it does provide tremendously reduced prices on the products it does carry.

- Don't miss the *Electronic Closeout/Special Sale Items* link at the bottom of the home page. You won't believe the high-quality, name-brand, new (never refurbished) products they offer. This page changes regularly—so check it often.

- Possibly one of the very best reasons to shop Sutter Telecom is their free shipping and handling policy.

Radar City

http://tribeca.ios.com/~cnsw/index.html

 Radar City sells everything from speakers to video cameras to telephones at unbeatable prices.

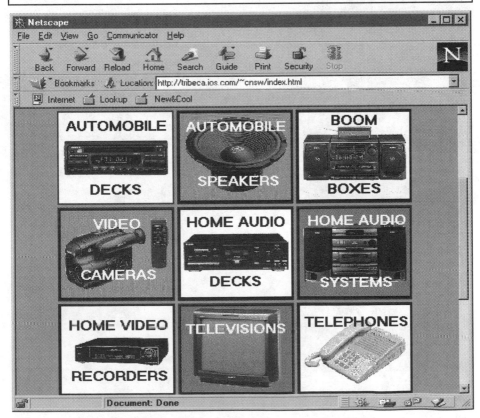

- Radar City is a no-frills bargain electronics Web site that guarantees to match any lower prices you find elsewhere.

- To place an order, click on a category link, determine the items you wish to purchase, and click on the *Order Form* link. There are no gimmicks or loud advertisements jumping off the page when you view this site. Its simplicity lets you get in and out of the site in a flash.

Camera Center

http://www.mall21.com/camera/

Camera Center promises to provide the lowest possible prices on many camera products.

- Camera Center is dedicated to camera bargains. A rare find on the Web, Camera Center is actually an offshoot of Mall21, a larger megasite.

- Camera Center sells complete cameras as well as individual camera parts for many leading brands. Check out the daily camera specials that are listed on the home page.

COMPUTERS

Multiwave

http://www.mwave.com/

This online superstore offers some of the lowest computer prices available on the Web.

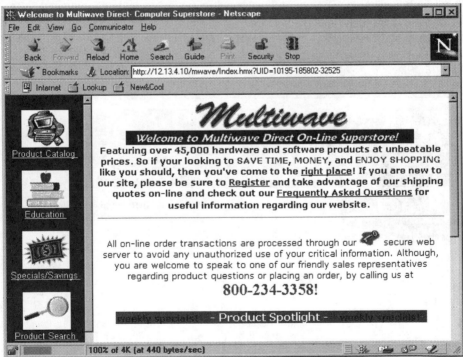

- Multiwave is a secure Web server that sells computers, computer peripherals, and software at rock-bottom prices. The Product Search page allows you to locate any computer-related product easily.

- Check out the Specials/Savings page for limited-time offers and hot deals on new products. This page also contains Blow Out Specials, which features manufacturer-refurbished products at deep discounts.

- Multiwave requires that you resister with their service prior to making your final purchase; however, this process is quick and easy.

MicroWarehouse

http://www.

 This popular mail-order store is now online, and offering special bargains to Web customers.

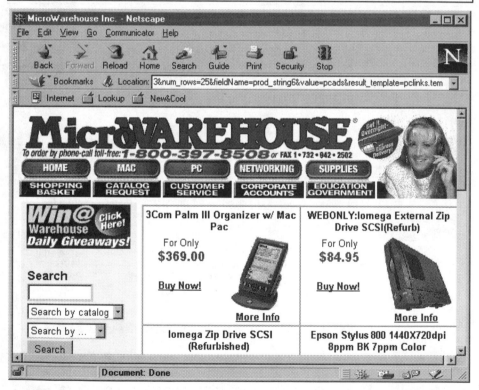

- Known for their variety and expansive stock, MicroWarehouse has long been one of the leading discount computer resellers.

- If you know what you're looking for, search by manufacturer, product name, or item number. Or, you can click on one of the numerous categories to locate the lowest prices for printers, computers, scanners, and other items.

NCBuy

http://www.ncbuy.com/computing/

 NCBuy carries an inventory of over 10,000 products, which allows the site to provide lower-than-average prices.

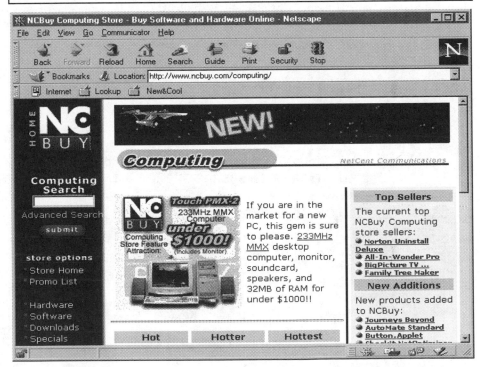

- NCBuy is simple, fast, and cheap. There is no need to spend time filling out detailed product information. Just type the product name or category into the Computing Search box on the NCBuy home page and you'll get a large and detailed list of applicable merchandise immediately.

- If you want a more detailed product search, click the *Advanced Search* link. This may take longer, but your results will be more refined.

Software

♦ Business, Graphics, and Home Use ♦ Educational
♦ Games, Multimedia, and Clip Art

From the latest word processing program to the coolest new computer game—the Internet is definitely the easiest and most cost-efficient way to get the software you need. From most sites software is often shipped overnight (or available for immediate download), is usually tax-free, and because there is little overhead it is often priced at 30–40% below retail.

BUSINESS, GRAPHICS, AND HOME USE

Software Clearance Outlet

http://www.softwareoutlet.com

For discounted educational children's software and reviews, this is the site to visit.

- Software Clearance Warehouse beats just about all retail prices for every type of software imaginable. They regularly sell software for as low as $2.00.

- The site is easy and fun to use. Just click on a software link and a list of applicable software titles and prices is displayed. For further details on a product, click the product link. A full-size picture displays along with a product review and product description report.

- Don't miss the *Specials* link, which connects you to a whole page of name-brand titles at pocket-change prices.

Software Street

http://www.softwarestreet.com/

This site carries over 10,000 software titles and specializes in business and desktop programs.

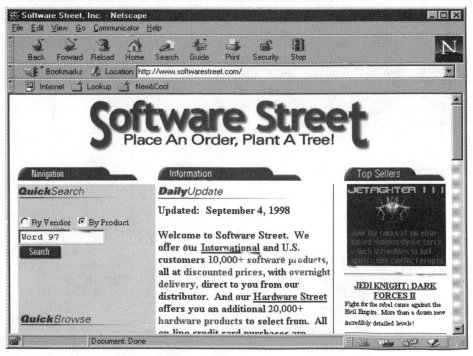

- Software Street is virtually a software powerhouse. Simply type the product or vendor you are seeking in the search box to generate a list of unbelievable volume at unimaginable prices. What's more, they promise to ship overnight and guarantee that over 95% of their merchandise is always in stock.

- Software Street also has a pact with the National Forest Foundation. Every time you make a purchase at their Web site, they'll make a contribution to planting a new tree in the forest.

Software Supermarket.com

http://www.softwaresupermaket.com

This site boasts over 100,000 products available for immediate download or next-day shipping.

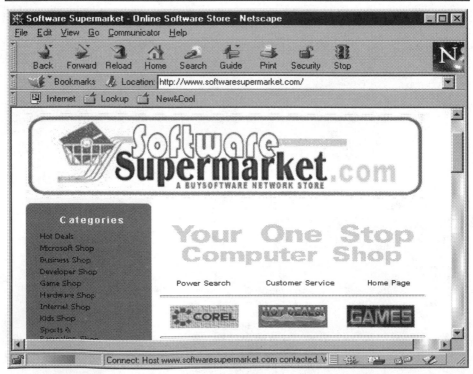

- You can find virtually everything you might need to make your computer operate for business, home, or fun at the Software Superstore.com Web site. In addition to thousands of discounted software titles, this site also has a "Download of the Week" feature, which allows you to purchase a software program online and download it immediately.
- Whatever you do, don't skip the *Hot Deals* link for incredible software titles and other computer-related products at bargain basement prices.

EDUCATIONAL

Smart Kids Software

http://www.smartkidssoftware.com/

This great site offers online educational materials as well as discounted software.

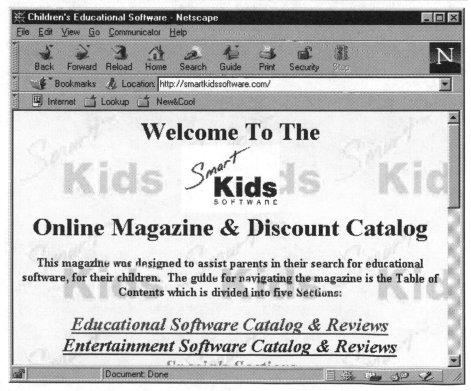

SOFTWARE

- Smart Kids Software is more than just a Web site that sells children's software. It's also an online magazine that contains product reviews and parental advice.

- Although all software titles at Smart Kids are largely discounted, you'll want to check out the Great Values link before making your final purchase. This section contains unbelievable mark-downs. Look for the red markings, which indicate free or drastically reduced items.

Kidtools

http://www.kidtools.com

This site is completely dedicated to children's software and educational tools.

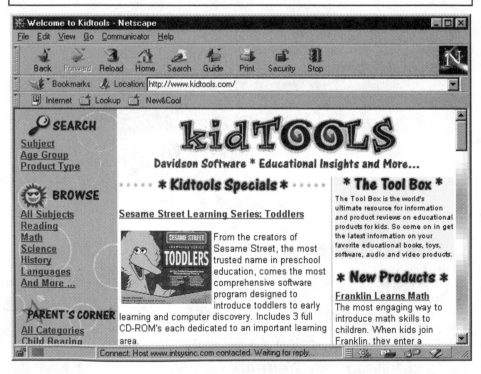

- KidTools provides software for younger computer users. All items are discounted and some are practically give-aways. And with categories such as foreign languages, history, reading, and math, you're sure to find something that interests and challenges every child.

- Use the KidTools search engine to search for software by subject, product type and age group. And don't miss the Parent's Corner section, which features family-related products for grown-ups .

The Edutainment Catalog Online

http://www.edutainco.com

This Web site provides education and entertainment software—all geared towards children.

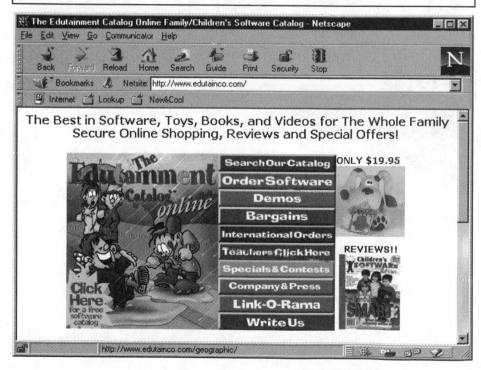

S
O
F
T
W
A
R
E

- A wonderful site for children (and parents) to visit, The Edutainment Catalog Online provides discounted children's educational software. In addition, they also sell toys, books, and videos with a family focus.
- Children can sign up for the free Birthday Club and receive a $5 coupon one month before their birthday. The site also provides contests, free demos of many software titles, and regularly updated bottom-dollar specials.

GAMES, CLIP ART, AND MULTIMEDIA

CD-ROM Cellar

http://www.cd-romcellar.com/

 Although this site occasionally offers business or graphics software, their real specialty is multimedia products and computer games.

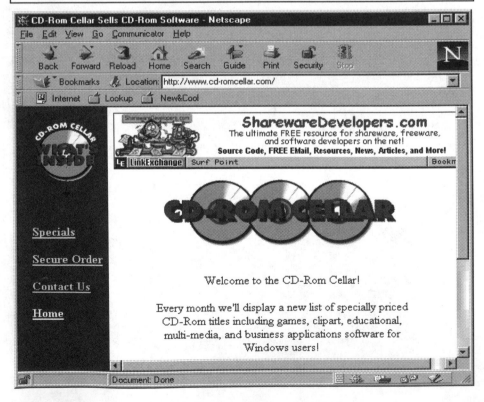

- This site functions as a software warehouse. Inventory comes and goes quickly and there's no guarantee that what you see today will be there tomorrow, so be sure to scoop up the good buys right when you find them.

- The CD-ROM Cellar's list of software titles changes monthly, so you may want to bookmark this site and check it out on a regular basis. You never know when they might be offering your favorite computer game for less than the price of a sandwich.

Up Front Multimedia

http://www.pacificnet.net/~upfront/

Up Front Multimedia offers specialized multimedia products for a wide range of topics.

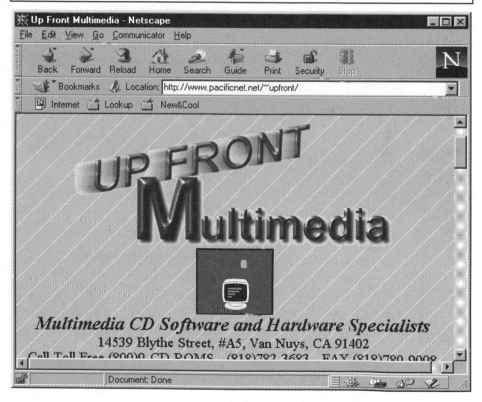

- Up Front Media specializes in multimedia products that cover such topics as education, business, children, entertainment, medical issues, and more. Some of their products teach, others just let you have fun, but all of them are offered at incredibly low prices with a promise that the company will not be undersold by anyone.

- Shopping at this site is easy. The best method is to browse by topic, then click a title to view more detailed information about the product. Or, you can review titles alphabetically if you already know the name of the product you're seeking.

Gameserve.com

http://www.gameserve.com

Gameserve.com carries over 10,000 computer games at up to 40% off retail value.

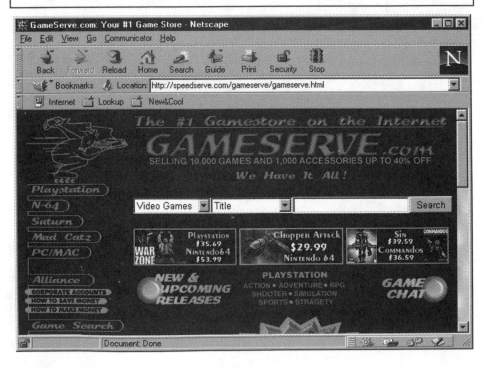

- Gameserve.com carries just about every computer and video game available on today's market. Most games are deeply discounted, often close to 40% of what you would pay elsewhere. The Gameserve.com search engine makes finding a game simple: type the title in the search box and press *Search* to display a description of the game, the platform on which it operates, and the current price.

- If you want to get really good at playing a particular game, click the *Tips and Tricks* link, which hooks you up with a Web page that describes the ins and outs of a particular game.

SOFTWARE

Toys & Hobbies

◆ Toys ◆ Hobbies

Looking for a rare baseball card, a new chess set, or the latest Beenie Baby? The Internet is a great place to search for such items. You'd be surprised how easy it is to find even the rarest collectibles at bargain prices—all from the comfort of your home.

TOYS

eToys™

http://www.etoys.com/

eToys is a giant online warehouse featuring every type of toy imaginable at the guaranteed lowest prices online.

- eToys carries everything from Barbie to Beanie Babies to backgammon—all with a 30-day price guarantee that will refund you 110% if you find the product advertised for less elsewhere.

- If eToys' regular prices aren't low enough for you, check out the 20 Under $20 section, which features 20 toys—for each age group—all for less than $20.

- If you're gift hunting but don't know what to buy, the Toy Search feature will help you find something by matching toy selections with criteria that you specify (age, category, price, etc.).

Toys"Я"Us

http://www.toysrus.com/

Yes, this national toy giant now offers it's incredible toy selection over the Internet—which means no more long lines at the store!

T
O
Y
S

- Toys"R"Us has always been known for their vast selection and great prices. If you've ever shopped at a "real world" Toys"R"Us store however, you know how easy it is to get lost—or merely exhausted—browsing through the seemingly endless isles of toys and games. But now you can experience this toy store giant without any of the inconvenience by using their powerful and easy online service. Simply select a shopping option (Departments, Featured Shops, or Gift Ideas) and then follow the simple online instructions to make your purchase.
- Don't miss out on the Great Deals link, which takes you to a Web page filled with bargain basement goodies.

ABC123 Toy Store

http://abc123.buysafe.com/

 The ABC123 Toy Store Web site features toys that are safe for younger children.

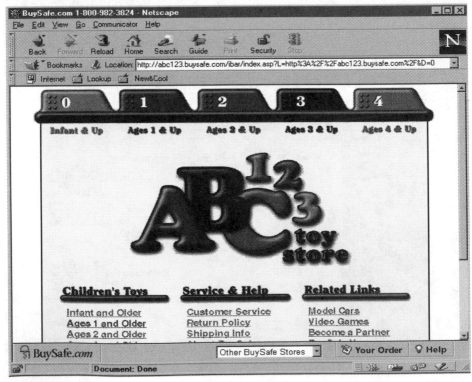

- As part of the BuySafe megasite, the ABC123 Toy Store offers a wide variety of toys for infants and young children at substantial discounts. Their customer satisfaction guarantees the best support on the Internet and shipping is always free.

- Just click on an age tab and choose a toy for a child in that age range. Click the BuySafe Model Cars or Video Games links to view more hobby and game related Web pages.

HOBBIES

Timeless Hobbies

http://www.timelesshobbies.com

This site offers rock-bottom prices on hobbies as well as toys. Their inventory is sure to surpass most "real world" hobby and game stores.

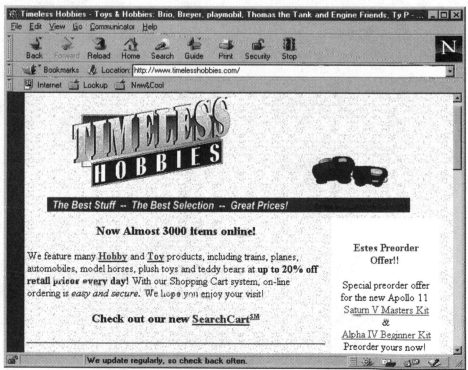

- With over 3,000 items in their inventory, Timeless Hobbies is the one-stop shopping center for most of your hobby and toy needs. From model rockets to model trains, they carry all the parts and pieces at prices that are close to 20% off of retail.

- Use the SearchCart search engine to search for hobby and toy items by price range, toy or hobby category, manufacturer and/or keywords. And the Fun Stuff link contains freebies, links to other cool sites, online greeting cards, and more.

Walden Hobbies

http://www.waldenhobbies.com/

 Walden Hobbies specializes in model trains in addition to selling various hobby materials and buying and selling collectable toys.

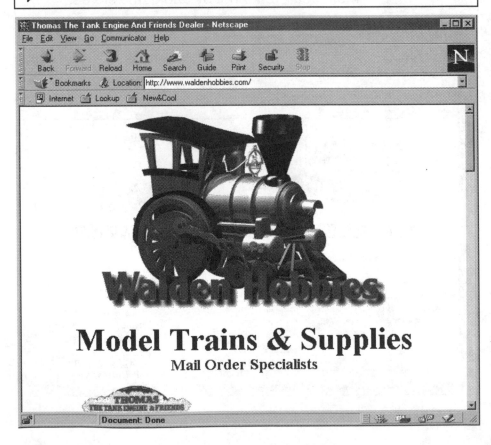

- If model trains are your game, then Walden Hobbies Web site is the place to be. Walden Hobbies is an authorized dealer for Thomas the Tank Engine products, which is a collectible line of model trains and train memorabilia.

- All items that are sold over the Internet are sold at a discounted rate. These rates are not available for non-Internet or mail order purchases.

Discount Magic Tricks and Pranks Store
http://www.discountmagic.com

This site carries everything you'd ever need to entertain your friends, host a magic theme party, or begin a career as a magician.

- This site carries everything from coin tricks to vanishing handkerchiefs to magic rings. Several items sell for less than $5 and all items are marked way below retail.

- If magic is a new hobby for you, check out the Books and Video section for discounted how-to books and videos. And don't miss the Pranks section, which is sure to make you a hit amongst co-workers and friends.

Sports & Leisure

◆ Garb & Gear ◆ The Great Outdoors ◆ Fitness
◆ Special Interests ◆ Other Sites

For every season, there's an activity, and for every activity, there's gear. Whether you like to have all the high-tech bells and whistles affiliated with a particular sport, or you just want a great deal on a new swimsuit, you can find it all online—and usually for less than what you'd pay at your local stores. Now you can outfit your whole family for the softball team *and* have enough cash left over for a new tent and hiking shoes, too. You just have to know where to look.

GARB & GEAR

gear.com

http://www.gear.com

 Gear.com can dress you up and gear you up for your favorite sport or activity.

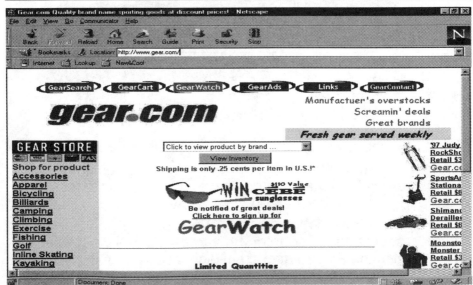

- Whether you want to paddle your own canoe, climb the highest mountain, or simply call it a day and just go fishing, step right up and get your gear—*all of it*—here. Gear.com has "screamin' deals" on brand-name manufacturer's overstocks.

- Search for items by manufacturer, sport, gear name, or description, and if you can't find it, you can request it. Register at the site for special customized services and hot tips on rock-bottom deals. This must-see site is safe and secure.

Sporting^{SM} Auction

http://www.sportingauction.com/

Bid on your favorite sport items at Sporting Auction—where you are bound to walk away with unbeatable deals.

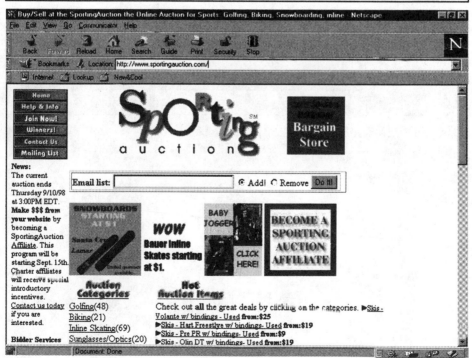

- If someone told you that you could buy inline skates and snowboards starting at $1.00, would you believe it? Come see for yourself at the Internet's only sporting-specific auction site.

- Bidding is safe and easy at this site, and if you're a little gun-shy, check out the *Winners!* link to see the winning bids on other items. Even if you don't want to participate in an auction, you can still save 30%–60% off fixed priced items in the Bargain Store. There's high turnaround at this site, so check frequently for new bargains.

Sportscape.com

http://www.sportscape.com

 Let Sportscape's powerful search engine find the discounted sport's equipment you need.

- Looking for good deals on hard-to-find items? This sports superstore has over 8,000 products in stock at 10%-120% below retail prices. This easy-to-browse site features hot sale items on the home page, and a complete search feature for all sporting accessories.

- Click the *On Sale!* link to save big bucks on closeout items. If you make a big purchase of $500 or more, you'll save an additional 5% off the bill. Enjoy safe and secure shopping and excellent customer service.

World Wide Sports®

http://www.1888wwsports.com

The World Wide Sports site offers great discounts everyday on bikes, skates, ski/snowboard equipment, hockey gear, clothing, uniforms, and more.

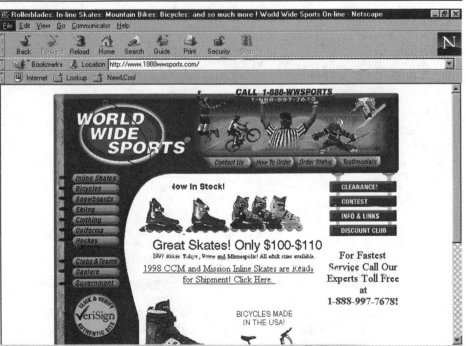

- Get notified via e-mail as soon as there's a sale on the sporting gear you want. That's one of the benefits of becoming a member of the World Wide Sports Discount Club.

- Have fun and participate in a monthly treasure hunt contest to win free gear, such as inline skates. All goods come with a 30-day return policy, and ordering is safe and secure.

THE GREAT OUTDOORS

TackleDIRECT.com

http://tackledirect.com

Reel in the best prices on rods, reels, leaders, terminals, and all your other fishing needs at this one-stop tackle site.

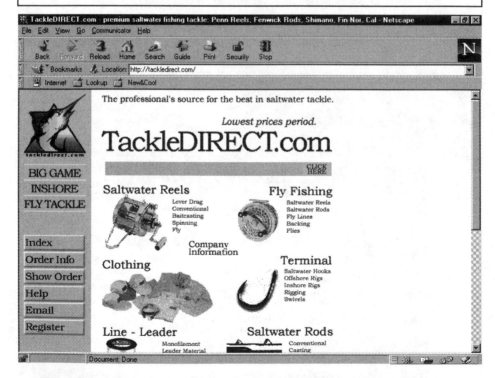

- The Great Outdoors Web site specializes in high-volume merchandise, so they can offer you the lowest prices on the best gear.

- Membership comes with additional benefits. New customers get a $50 bonus, plus free gift certificates, free shipping, and free line. Search hundreds of categories for thousands of products and make safe and secure purchases.

REI-Outlet.com

http://www.rei-outlet.com

Get the best outdoor gear and clothing at REI's exclusive online Bargain Outlet.

- Serious outdoor enthusiasts would do well to bookmark this site for rock-bottom prices on overstocks, closeouts, and seconds. Items are limited, so your best bet is to check this site frequently.

- If you want a specific item, you can get the Bargain Sleuth to find it for you and notify you when it's available. Get everything from camping gear, to kids' stuff, to car racks. All goods are guaranteed with a 30-day return policy, and shopping is secure.

Outdoor World of California

http://www.outdoorworlddca.com

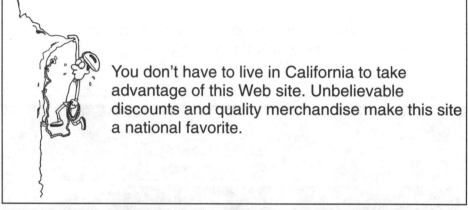

You don't have to live in California to take advantage of this Web site. Unbelievable discounts and quality merchandise make this site a national favorite.

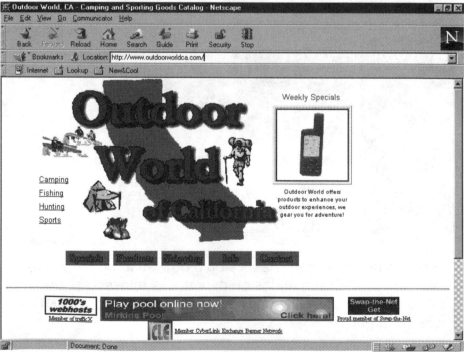

- You'll find weekly specials at this site for all your favorite outdoor activities, including camping, fishing, hunting, and other recreational sports.

- Click the *Specials* link on the home page to get 20%, 30%, 50% and more off retail prices for everything from scopes to sleeping bags to snorkels. Call or fax orders toll free. New items are discounted every week, so check often for new deals.

FITNESS

FitnessNet

http://www.fitnessnet.com

Let your gym come to you! Fitness Net delivers brand-name equipment straight to your door.

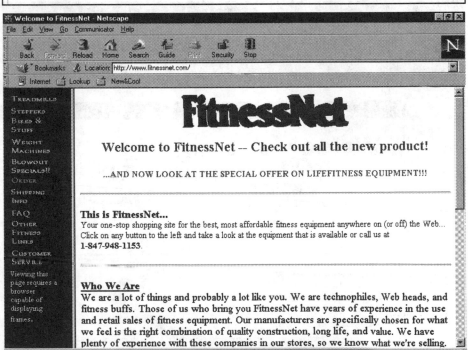

- If you're looking to burn calories at home without burning a hole in your credit card, you can save hundreds of dollars off of high-end fitness equipment at FitnessNet.

- For treadmills, weight machines, stationary bikes, and steppers, this may be the cheapest source on the Internet. Click the *Blowout Specials* link to save 10% off of already marked down prices.

- At this point and time you may not want to submit your credit card information because they don't have a secure server, but you can place orders through their 800 line.

FitnessZone

http://www.fitnesszone.com

The Fitness Zone offers discounted workout equipment as well as newsletters, apparel, tanning supplies and more.

- Want to get in shape? No sweat! FitnessZone is dedicated to bringing you the best prices on the highest quality fitness and health merchandise. Get everything from cardiovascular equipment to saunas to apparel at hundreds of dollars off retail prices.

- This informative site also has excellent customer service and a 30-day, 100% refund policy on all items. Become a member for additional benefits including fitness forums, free e-zines, and free classifieds.

SPECIAL INTERESTS

International Golf Outlet, Inc.
http://www.igogolf.com

If golf is your game, don't miss online golf outlet site.

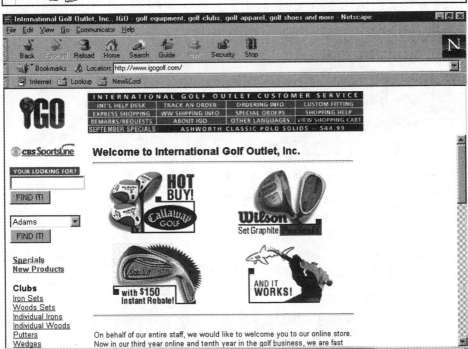

- If you want clubs, balls, books, aids, apparel, and accessories, IGO is bound to have it, and at discount prices. Check out the monthly specials for bargain barrel sales, request specific items, and even get free custom fitting, based on criteria you enter about yourself.

- This site has thousands of items in stock, and new hot discount items are added every few weeks. At this golf lovers' megasite, you'll find exceptional customer service that continues well beyond your date of purchase.

Play Pro

www.playpro.com

This site specializes in tennis, racquetball, and squash making it easier, and less expensive to find everything you need for your sport in one location.

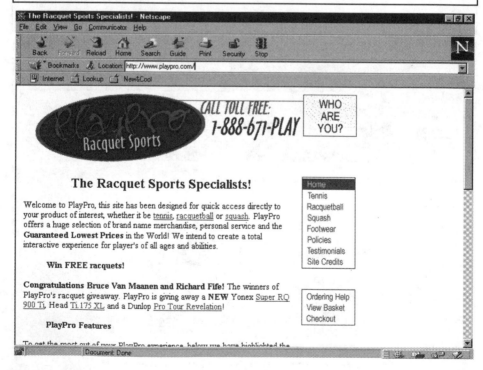

- Tennis anyone? Or do you prefer racquetball or squash? Whatever your racquet, Play Pro has a tremendous selection of brand-name products, shoes, and services at "the lowest prices in the world" guaranteed. That means if you find a better deal, they'll match it, and with better service, too.

- Other great features include free professional stringing (with the string of your choice) and free items with purchases, including videos, socks, gloves, bags, and more bags. You'll soon discover why this site has gotten tons of rave reviews.

Internet Cue Store

http://www.cuestore.com

 The Internet Cue Store promises to stock virtually every cue there is—in addition to countless other discounted billiard products.

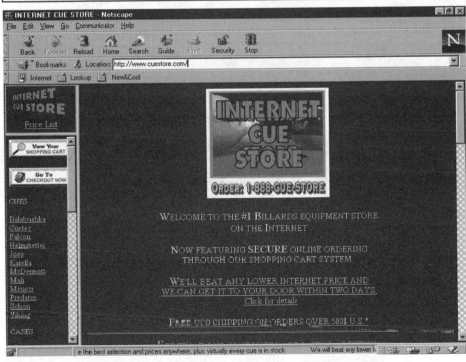

- Whether your game is straight, eight-ball, nine-ball, or snooker, you're bound to find all your favorite cues, cases, tables, and billiard accessories at the Internet Cue Store—and all at discount prices.

- For a quick peek at all items, click the *Price List* link and compare this site's prices with the suggested retail to see how much you'll save. This site promises to beat any price you find on the Internet, and have the package on your doorstep within two days. And, if you spend more than $500, shipping fees are on the house.

Beach Bowl Pro Shop

http://www.beachbowlproshop.com

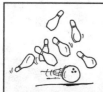 If bowling is up your alley, be sure to check out this fun and browser-friendly site for the lowest possible prices on bowling balls, bags, shoes, and accessories.

- In addition to great prices, you'll get free finger inserts with ball purchases, and free shipping with all your orders. Be sure to click the *Specials* link for factory seconds that are lower than auction prices.

- Explore the Beach Bowl Pro Shop to find the bowling ball or bowling accessory that's right for you. A color photo and detailed description is provided for each item.

The Fun-Attic

http://www.funattic.com

For unique outdoor items and gifts, the reasonably priced Fun-Attic Web site is the place to visit.

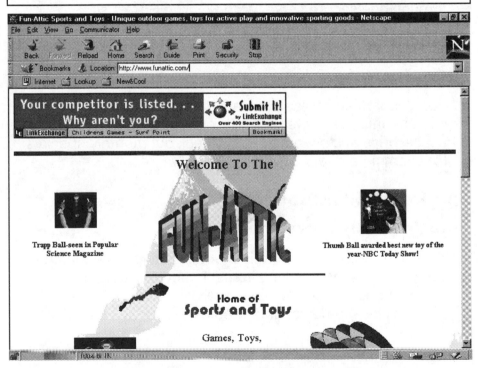

- If you're looking for fling socks, thumb balls, kites, or non-slip mega-grip balls, look no further. The Fun-Attic is the mother of all sites for unique outdoor toys, games, and sporting goods.

- Although this isn't a discount site, you can find specialty items that you won't find elsewhere, and the prices are reasonable. The Fun-Attic also offers free game instructions, ideas, school fundraiser help, and great links to sites that specialize in items for kids and disabled athletes .

OTHER SITES

Online Sports

http://www.onlinesports.com/

- Whether you're a couch potato sports enthusiast or a peak-performance athlete wannabe, you're bound to find *all* sport-related goods at this extensive site. Search for specific items in virtually all sporting-related categories, and buy online through one secure server at the Online Sports site.

The Action Sports Exchange

http://www.fmz.com

- For all board enthusiasts, whether its for snow, surf, or cement, this site offers tons of brand-name boards and accessories at blow-out prices. Check out monthly specials for even more deals.

The Roller Warehouse

http://www.rollerwarehouse.com

- This site is a skaters' paradise for all skating, rollerblading, hockey, and speed skating items. In addition to regular discount prices, you can save even more with featured specials, insane deals, and freebies.

Travel

◆ Air, Car, and Cruise ◆ Lodging

Now you can become your own travel agent! The same
information that is available to your local travel agent is also
available on the Web. You can book your own air, car, cruise,
hotel—you name it! You can easily search for the best rates,
best times, and best packages by simply plugging in your
desired itinerary.

AIR, CAR, AND CRUISE

Internet Travel Agency

http://www.InternetTravelAgency.com/

ITA is a one-stop reservation specialist that
books reservations for everything from cruises,
to rental cars, to airline tickets.

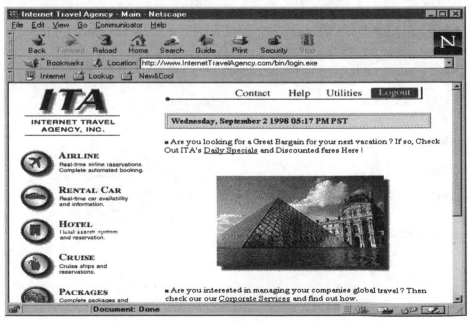

- ITA is quick and thorough. Once you log in (only an e-mail address and name are required), you can click on a desired mode or method of travel (airline, rental car, hotel, cruise, or packages), punch in where you want to go, and a list of options displays within seconds.

- Click the *Daily Specials* link to view frequently updated rock-bottom travel discounts.

- Each travel link has a Shopper feature which allows you to view the cheapest rates for your given destination. To find out if those rates are available, click the *reservation* link and supply your projected itinerary.

Online Fares Travel

http://www.onlinefares.com/

 Online Fares Travel is currently dedicated exclusively to air travel.

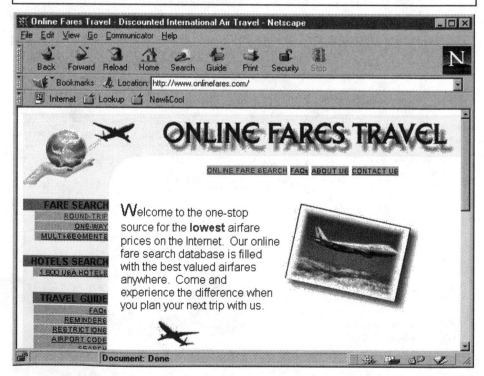

- Although it currently sells only tickets for international air travel, this is one of the quickest and easiest Web travel sites to use. In a matter of seconds you can locate the cheapest flight to Paris, buy the tickets, and be on your way.

- Click the *Hot Deals* link on the home page to view unbeatable short notice discounts.

Yahoo! Travel

http://www.travel.yahoo.com/

 Yahoo!, the popular Web search engine, contains a travel site which is one of the Web's easiest and fastest to use.

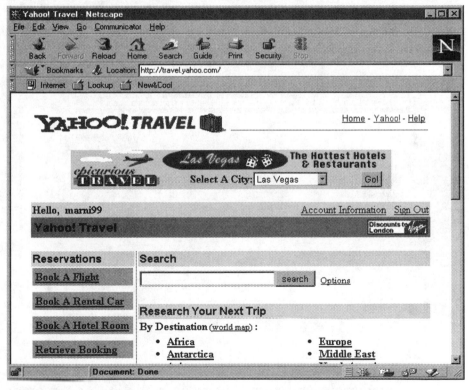

- One of the best features of Yahoo! Travel is that you don't have to sign in to get up-to-the-minute price and travel information for air, car, hotel, cruise, or package deals. In the long run, this saves you a lot of searching time.

T
R
A
V
E
L

- The *Travel Bargains* link from the home page provides information about airline specials (such as free or low-priced companion fares) and unbelievable last-minute travel opportunities.

BizTravel.com

http://www.travel.yahoo.com/

 Biztravel isn't just for business travelers. Anyone creating a detailed travel itinerary should check out this sophisticated travel site.

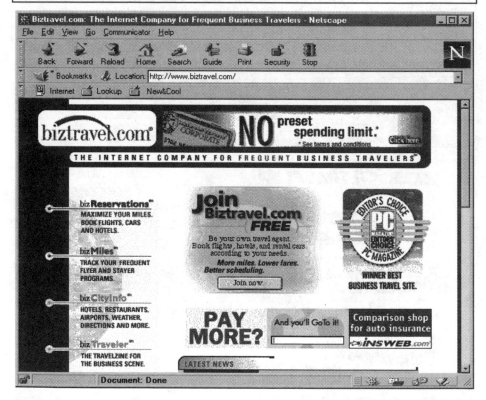

- Biztravel.com functions like a true travel agent by searching all the same databases that a travel agent searches. Once you supply your name, e-mail address, and Zip Code in order to register, you can book all your travel plans from one screen. That means no jumping from airline link to hotel link to car rental link!

- As biztravel.com busily combs the Web for the best prices matching your itinerary, a window explaining the status of your search displays. The window shows you which hotels, airlines, etc., the database has searched for availability.

- Be sure to check out the *Latest News* section of the home page, which informs you of pending travel issues and great discounts.

LODGING

Bed & Breakfast Inns Online

http://www.bbonline.com

This specialized site caters to folks all over the country who want to find a "get away" in a cozy environment.

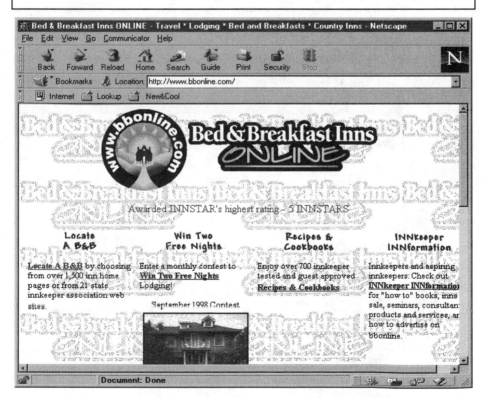

- Bed & Breakfast Inn Online proudly features over 1,500 bed and breakfast locations across the Unites States. Instead of thumbing through countless books to locate a remote B&B, now you can simply click on the region you wish to visit and choose a link to a desired B&B.

- Although you can't sort the B&B's by price to locate the best deals, you will notice that most locations offer discount rates with certain restrictions. In addition, the Bed and Breakfast Inns Online home page offers discounts on a regular basis.

1 800 USA HOTELS.com

http://www.1800usahotels.com/

1 800 USA HOTELS.com can locate discount rates for hotels, bed and breakfast lodging, and spas.

- Possibly the most diverse lodging site on the Web, 1 800 USA HOTELS.com promises to find low national and international rates. The site provides detailed information about each location, as well as pictures when available. In addition, the Hotel section allows you to sort for availability by price.

- A favorite feature of this site is the frequent flier program, which allows you to accrue miles for each reservation you book through the service. Also, be sure to check out the *Monthly Specials* and *Spotlight* on the home page, which contain bonus discounts.

Roomfinders.com

http://www.roomfinders.com/

Roomfinders.com brings you the lowest possible hotel rates in most designated areas.

- Roomfinders.com locates hotels within major cities and locations throughout the country. Simply select a destination from the pull-down menu and Roomfinders.com will display a list of possibilities within the area.
- Click *Special Deals* to view bottom-dollar hotel rates at special locations.

Innroads

http://www.inns.com/

 Innroads provides detailed listings for over 1,500 lodging sites around the U.S. and Canada.

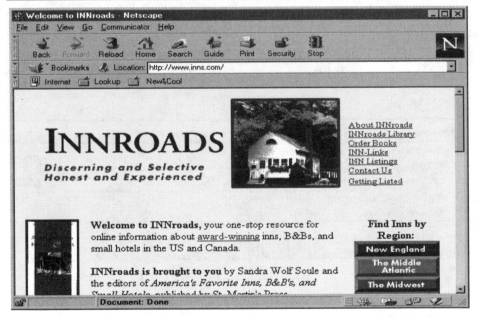

- If you're looking for a quaint getaway, this is the place to start. The Innroads site provides the details for each inn listed, including room description, amenities, nearby shops, and activities. In addition, an inn's picture can help seal the deal. Just click on a region and browse the selections.
- The home page even provides information on becoming an innkeeper yourself. And the *Innroads Library* link provides online newsletters that feature articles on various inns and inn-related topics.

Index

O

P

R

S

NEW at ddcpub.com!

Visit the DDC Web Rover Gallery
Go to www.ddcpub.com
and click on the *Web Rover Gallery* link

The **DDC Web Rover** hunts the Internet every week, sniffing out the best sites on the Web.

In the **DDC Web Rover Gallery**, you'll find links to great Web Rover recommended resources for students, bargain hunters, sales people, managers, seniors. You'll also find great entertainment, leisure, and vacation sites.

If you are on the scent of a Web site you find interesting, DDC would like to hear from you. Click on the Web Rover's link and submit the site and the reason you like it. If we list it in the Gallery, you'll receive a free Computer and Internet dictionary.*

We search the Web so you don't have to!

*This is a limited time offer.